THE GARDENS OF SCOTLAND

The Gardens of Britain
Advisory Editor: D. J. Sales,
*Gardens Adviser to the National
Trust of England and Wales*

THE GARDENS OF SCOTLAND

Peter Verney

B. T. BATSFORD LTD   *London*

Computer typeset by
Input Typesetting Ltd, London SE1
Printed in Great Britain by
Biddles Ltd, Guildford, Surrey
for the Publishers
B. T. Batsford, 4 Fitzhardinge St, London W1H 0AH

CONTENTS

ACKNOWLEDGMENT

I would like to express my deep and sincere appreciation for the very great help I have received from many quarters in the preparation of this book. In particular to:– Major and Mrs Michael Crichton Stuart for Falkland Palace; The Marquess of Ailsa for Culzean; Lieutenant-Colonel A. N. Balfour of Dawyck; Mr James Burnett of Leys for Crathes Castle; Lady Jean Fforde for Brodick; Mr Stewart Annand for Branklyn; The Earl and Countess of Haddington for Tyninghame; Mr William Edgar for Doune and Mr W. R. Hean for Threave. I only hope that I have done justice in these pages to the lovely gardens which they, and in some cases their forebears have created.

I would also like to thank Mr Peter Stageman and his staff at the Library of the Royal Horticultural Society in Vincent Square for the invaluable advice and assistance they afforded me in my research.

But my deepest gratitude must go to the National Trust for Scotland and in particular Mrs Jean Baines – for their help in many directions and the most generous loan of photographs.

For permission to reproduce photographs the Author and Publisher would like to thank the National Trust for Scotland for plates 3-9, 13, 14 (photographer, W. S. Scott), 17, 18 and 20; the British Travel and Holidays Association for plate 10. The remainder come from the Author's collection. All the colour plates were kindly lent by The National Trust for Scotland and Christopher K. Milne.

Special thanks are due to Miss Elizabeth Simmons for the plans of the gardens and to Chartwell Illustrators for the decorative line drawings.

LIST OF PHOTOGRAPHS

GARDEN PLANS

The Gardens of Scotland

1 Abercairny
2 Achamore House
3 An Cala
4 Ardanaiseig
5 Ardwell House
6 Calgary House
7 Craignish Castle
8 Crarae Lodge
9 Drummond Castle
10 Edinburgh Royal Botanic Gardens
11 Glenarn
12 Hopetoun House
13 Keir
14 Kildrummy Castle Gardens
15 Kinmount
16 Leith Hall
17 Lochinch and Castle Kennedy Gardens
18 Logan Botanic Gardens
19 Malleny
20 Pollok Park
21 Scone Palace
22 Strone
23 The House on the Shore
24 Williamston
25 Younger Botanic Gardens

FOREWORD

by John Sales, Gardens Adviser to the National Trust of England and Wales

The British Isles hold horticultural riches unparalleled elsewhere. No area of the world can offer to the curious such a diversity of gardens, plants and styles of landscape design within a few hundred miles; all open to visitors and expressing so much of the culture of the country and horticultural skill of the people.

Every individual sees a garden with different eyes and, according to his interests, appreciates one aspect or another. The purpose of this series is to introduce gardens to the visitor and to help him to grasp more fully their intrinsic qualities; the better to enrich his understanding and deepen his experience.

Gardeners soon find that there is more to it than assembling together the greatest number of the largest and most colourful, or even the rarest plants, although a great deal of pleasure can be had from seeing any plant well grown. The 'collectors' interest in gardening should not be underestimated and many great gardens have begun on this basis. But the potential range of plants is so wide that sooner or later selection becomes inevitable. Sometimes a built-in discipline is imposed by extremes of site or soil, often with unifying results, but in most cases the owner has made a conscious selection according to his preference and the taste of the day.

Clearly then, gardens can be statements of a particular personality or, more frequently, the expression of two in combination, e.g. designer and interested client or husband and wife. Sometimes a garden will show the imprint of a succession of generations of one family, each changing or adding a little, and give evidence of the remarkable continuity in the ownership of great houses and gardens throughout the centuries, which is so rare elsewhere and so relatively common in Britain.

Styles of gardening have undergone enormous changes with the ebb and flow of civilization and cultural ideals on the one hand, and changes in internal security and social structures on the other.

It is axiomatic that the older the style the less likely it is to survive but some gardens still retain the outlines of mediaeval enclosures, which would have contained their orchards and knot gardens. From these it is possible to trace the development of garden style from the formal layouts of the 16th and 17th centuries, through the English Landscape style of the 18th century and the self-confident eclecticism of the Victorians, to the carefully contrived colour schemes of the 20th century.

The comparatively equable climate of the British Isles and the enormous variety of habitat has enabled us to grow a wider range of plants outside than anywhere else in the world. It is partly for this reason but also because of our long tradition of scientific exploration and plant collecting that we enjoy such richness and diversity of plants in our gardens, a heritage which is now being eroded by shrinking plant catalogues and commercial pressures.

The series 'Gardens of Britain' is attempting a task never before undertaken; to provide eventually descriptions of all the major gardens open to visitors throughout Great Britain and Ireland. Separate authors will deal with each of the several regions and, except for the first, each volume will be comprehensive for the area it covers. For every garden there will be sufficient factual information to be of value to the serious visitor and student but the main aim will be to give a clear picture of the garden and its plants; to whet the appetite before a visit, to guide at the time and to enjoy in retrospect.

Garden lovers in Britain will in due course and for the first time have available a reference book for the increasingly popular pastime of garden visiting, not only for their own and neighbouring counties but also for any area they may choose for a holiday. Already garden visitors number hundreds of thousands annually and large sums are raised for charity and for the maintenance of gardens by generous owners. With the parallel growth of interest in gardening the series fills an obvious gap and will form a unique record for posterity.

It is appropriate that the series should begin in so rich a field as Scotland, home of so many great gardens and gardeners. In the first volume Peter Verney has written with his usual authority a lively account of some of the more important Scottish gardens. His is a distinctly personal and refreshing approach, tracing the history of gardening north of the border through his own selection of gardens.

D. J. SALES

INTRODUCTION

WHAT MAKES a garden? Is it the plants? Is it the place? Is it the personality of those who created it? Or is it, as I believe, a magical blend of all three?

Certainly in some of the gardens I describe in these pages, the strength of personality of their creators lives on – Osgood Mackenzie and Mairi Sawyer at Inverewe, the Burnett of Leys at Crathes, the Rentons at Branklyn, and what must be an almost unique case on the British gardening scene, the succession of three quite unrelated families, each in their time near the forefront of horticulture, who over the span of three centuries created the gardens at Dawyck.

But would the gardens be what they are today without their natural settings and often the framework of old walls? I doubt it. For gardening is the most ephemeral of arts. After a few years nothing may be left of a garden it took a decade to make. The hours of planning and heart-searching; the delicious agony of wondering if a plant is in the right place, is of the right type and with the right companions; the triumph, when something not only survives, but thrives, when, by all gardening precepts, it should have withered and died; the vagaries of a fickle climate. All the results of years of toil can be swept into near-oblivion under an impenetrable jungle of weeds in a matter of a few seasons.

Even the scenes created by the great landscape designers of former centuries, Wise, 'Capability' Brown, Repton, Kent and others, may change, as gaps begin to appear in the treescapes they were at such pains to create, and death, disease and high winds take their toll. Or unthinking planting in a place deliberately left open may undermine the strength of the original composition. Weeds and mud may silt up a piece of water whose chief impact may have rested on reflection or contrast. Would, then, the original landscape artist recognise his work?

Thus, when the original creator passes away, inevitably, a garden starts to lose its individual character. Plants outgrow their positions, hedges start to dwarf and smother those they should protect. Sooner or later every garden reaches a form of change of life and it is then, when the subsequent replanting must take place, that the loss of identity occurs. One misses, and can immediately detect, the loss of the original artistry of the former creator who gardened in the idiom of the time; the plant association, the grouping, the innate knowledge through years of experience of which plant is right, and which is wrong. For a garden must be a personal creation. How greatly therefore it is to the credit of the National Trust, the National Trust for Scotland, in particular the Trust's Gardens' Adviser Mr Eric Robson and other public bodies in these islands that they have been able to preserve so much of the individual character of the fine gardens they have inherited and now hold in their care.

And of the plants? They must speak for themselves. But behind many plants lurks the romance of their discovery and behind every gardener is the spirit of the great plant-collectors of the last centuries – so many of them, as it happens, Scottish – even if the manifestation of this is confined to sponge-bag warfare with the Customs.

It is this blend of personalities, of the place in which they have been created, and of course the plants, that I have tried to find in each of the twelve gardens I describe in this book.

Any selection is certain to be invidious. Those knowledgeable of the Gardens of Scotland will ask, 'Where is Crarae?' 'There's no mention of Glenarn, or Kier, or Ardnaseig – except in a brief appendix?' 'What about Abercairny, Glena and Kildrummill?' 'Can any book on Scottish gardens exclude, except in passing reference, Achamore on the Island of Gigha, that island paradise created by the late Sir John Horlick off the coast of Kintyre, in Argyll?'

But a selection is also personal. The choice of gardens in this book has been exclusively my own. It has been dictated, partly because I have selected gardens which are open to the public for the greater part of the season and which annually attract the greatest number of visitors; partly because I have endeavoured to cover as representative a cross-section of the many types of garden, and of garden fashion, that there are in Scotland – from the west coast lushness of Brodick Castle and Inverewe, to the chill airs of Dawyck; from the genius at Crathes Castle to the high planting talent at Tyninghame; and partly because in those I write about I can reflect the development of Scottish Gardening History and a particular gardening style.

For many of these gardens can be directly associated with, or owe their origin or development to, certain periods in the evolution of the Scottish Garden. Within the old walls of Falkland Palace it is not hard to visualise the mediaeval garden. At Pitmedden, although the modern planting scheme has none of the muted elegance of the old form, nonetheless, the parterre form of gardening, the formality of the seventeenth-century garden is well displayed. The Victorian mould is represented at Kellie Castle. The rock garden *par excellence* at Branklyn, and so on.

However, to make amends to those other, and some very beautiful gardens which are open regularly, or for extended periods throughout the season, and which are neglected in these pages, I have included brief reference in an appendix; and their location is shown on the map in italics. For those other gardens in Scotland, which are occasionally open to the public, the reader's attention is drawn to a publication entitled *Scotland's Gardens,* which is on sale at tourist offices, bookshops and most hotels in Scotland. This is an essential companion for anyone interested in the great wealth, and diversity of the Gardens in Scotland.

ONE

Falkland Palace *Fife*

THE EARLIEST recorded gardens in Scotland are those of the monasteries and ecclesiastical orders. Few details have passed down to us and few traces remain today, but there is no doubt that these centres of agriculture – for that is what they really were – possessed fine orchards and herbaries. Many of the religious foundations were vast landowners and their influence on their own tenants and on the general husbandry in their areas was considerable. Not only did the monks provide physic from their herb gardens for the community around, but they also gave advice on agricultural practice. Their ideas were often well ahead of their time.

But these monastic gardens were largely utilitarian; the first garden in Scotland devoted, at least in part, to pleasure, was in all probability at Stirling Castle, one of the palaces of the Royal House of Stewart. Traces of this garden exist today, and it is believed that the Knot Garden at Stirling may have existed as long ago as 1450. Substantial alterations were evidently put in hand in 1497 by one Schir John Sharp, the King's chaplain; a versatile cleric who also laid out the garden at Holyroodhouse in Edinburgh. Records also reveal that there were gardens at the other royal residences of Linlithgow Palace and on the Castle Rock in Edinburgh, at Elgin and at Roxburgh and Jedburgh in the Borders. Of these nothing remains, but at Falkland in the fertile countryside of Fife, it is not difficult to visualise how the old Stewart garden may have looked.

Set beneath the peaceful Lomonds, in sight of the twin 'Paps of Fife', Falkland Palace presides over the small township of Falkland. Built as a hunting lodge, here generations of Stewarts enjoyed their sport and found time to relax. The Forest of Falkland, of which nothing remains today, abounded in deer, to the dismay of the local people who saw their crops ravaged by the animals, often without redress. When the royal chase was done, the hunters returned to the palace.

For nearly two centuries the Stewarts made Falkland their hunting palace. Stewart history is characterised by tragedy and sudden death; Falkland has seen its share. For here David Stewart, Duke of Rothesay, son of King Robert III of Scotland, died under mysterious circumstances while a prisoner in 1402; James V died here in 1542, of a broken heart it was said, leaving his kingdom to the tragic, beautiful and ill-fated Mary Queen of Scots; Charles II, the Merry Monarch of later years, quitted Falkland in 1651, bound for defeat and exile.

Though the old walls have seen sorrow enough, it is as a place of gaiety that one likes to think of Falkland. Here Mary Queen of Scots before her capture and eventual execution, romped and laughed and 'played the country girl' in its parks and woods. In the gardens beneath the Palace courtiers practised their archery in the 'lang butts', ran races or played tennis in the Royal Tennis Court or 'catch-spiel', which is one of the oldest in the British Isles. The halls and chambers rang with laughter and revelry, and poets and musicians came to recite and play at one of the most cultured courts in Europe. Thus of pageants, masques, sport and dalliance Falkland has seen plenty, and it is not hard to understand why the old palace was so beloved by the Stewarts. Here was their country home where for a few stolen moments it was possible to forget the tribulations that tormented their wild and turbulent kingdom.

A feature of the Stewart court were the animals. Not just the Lion of Scotland, royal mascot to the House of Stewart, which accompanied his master wherever he went, but more lovable playmates; a pet fox, the parrots – one of the Royal servants was even called the Keeper of the Parrot – and a performing seal.

A castle is known to have existed at Falkland as early as 1120, but the building that stands today all dates from the first half of the sixteenth century. The old records reveal many details; how the stone was brought down from the nearby Lomonds by sledge, but that for the gargoyles and paving had to come from Angus because it was more durable. That timber for the most part came from the Park of Falkland except for Swedish oak and fir which was widely

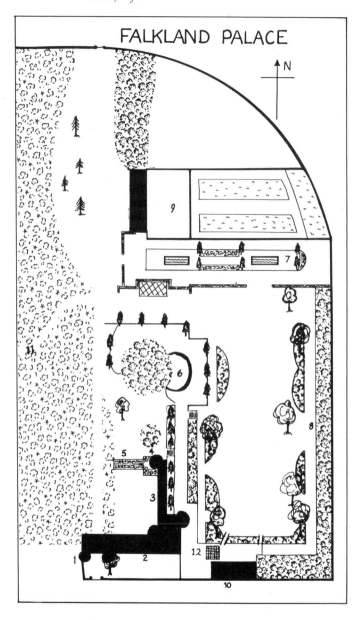

FALKLAND PALACE

N

1. Gate House
2. South Range
3. East Range
4. North Range
5. Rose Garden
6. Remains of old Castle
7. Water Garden
8. The Great Border
9. Tennis Court
10. East Port : Reception Centre
11. Old orchard
12. Draughts Board

used; while wood for the scaffolding came, surprisingly, from as far afield as Rouen in France.

First to be built was the North Range – on the site of what is now the Rose Garden. Here was the Great Hall, a place for formal entertainments and banquets. Huge oriel windows lighted the high table where the King's Chair of State was placed; a massive hammer-beam roof was believed to have covered all. But, in 1654 tragedy struck, for, on '3 September, being the Sabbath, att night a pairt of the palace of Falkland nearest the garden yearde was brunt; at this time a garrison of the English was leyen there'. And evidently Cromwell's troops, for that is who they were, had been making themselves very comfortable from the evidence of the orders for 'coals'. The roof was partially destroyed and the rest soon decayed. Finally the walls were used as a quarry by the neighbourhood and many of the stones of the old North Range are moulded into the walls of the older houses in the town – from time to time they still come to light.

Of a later date, are the East and South Ranges, constructed in the time of James IV in the early sixteenth century and embellished during the reign of James V. On the south, the street side, stands as fine a piece of ancient Scottish architecture as survives today; but on the north side, overlooking the Courtyard, the King's French 'wrichts' (wrights) and masons have created what Mark Girouard in *Country Life* described as a 'display of early Renaissance architecture wthout parallel in the British Isles'.

Domestic and political instability over the centuries has largely dictated the style of architecture in Scotland. Even at Falkland, which was primarily a country retreat, the need for some protection is evident in the design of the South Range where Holy statues vie with barred windows and battlements, while loopholes overlook the high street of Falkland town, the 'Fortress of Fyfe'.

First mention of the gardens at Falkland is in 1456 when it is noted in the Palace Rolls that wages for a gardener had been paid but were later withdrawn and the man dismissed, as they were found to be 'undeserved'. Then in 1484 instructions are left that a gardener should be paid on condition that he works well and provides the king with eight barrels of onions each year. Whether the garden at Falkland was comparable with that at Stirling must remain a matter for conjecture – although it is probable, as for many years the two

Falkland Palace: the Upper Paving.

palaces shared the same gardener – but certainly in the latter were
to be found leeks and kail as well as pears, 'plowms', willows and
vines. Apart from the vegetable garden, it is probable that an
orchard too existed at Falkland for the remains of old trees were
found during excavations to the north-west of the present Palace and
fruit trees have been replanted on the old site – a gentle, south-facing
slope. Little is known of the Pleasure Garden or Pleasance which
must have existed, but there is reference to a door being constructed
in 1461 so that James II's widow might be able to walk from her
chamber to the lawn and garden; and some fifty years later, when an
item in the Rolls authorises payment for the removal of a 'rough
wooden trellis' and its replacement by stone walls.

This would lead one to suppose that the garden at Falkland –

although there are no records to support the contention – was typical of the time: strictly formal in appearance, essentially inward-looking and probably rectangular or square – a reflection of the *Hortus Conclusus* of Roman days. There was little attempt then to incorporate the features of the country around, or to harmonise with the landscape. This was in part considered too cheerless; in part it was an echo of the mood of the owner who sought a haven sheltered both physically and spiritually from the harsh, unattractive world outside.

In all probability the garden would have been divided into enclosures, square or rectangular as well, each surrounded by trellis or low hedges. Within the enclosures, some of which might be raised, would be small 'knotte' gardens, with low hedges of hyssop, thyme, lavender or rue around other plants or coloured earths. Or a fountain, sundial or other ornament to delight the on-looker. And in the garden would be found the common flowers of the day, for the most part indigenous, but some brought back by travellers from Europe or even the Near East – the gilliflower or carnation; the auriculas or bears-ears; peonies; poppies; wallflowers; roses; violets and others, including, perhaps some more recently introduced from France, like the French sorrel or the angelica.

And there would be arbours – 'Shadowe-houses' they were called and walks. One known as the Gilderland Walk commemorates Mary of Gilderland, the same lady who had a door constructed between her chamber and the garden. The Gilderland walk leads between two clumps of trees known locally as the Queen's Quarrels, which may once have been hardwoods and provided the quarrels, or arrows, for cross-bows. Probably west of the stables, near the present stream, was the stank or stew-pond. It was stocked with pike, trout and lampreys, all presumably living in perfect, and peculiar, sixteenth-century harmony.

Next mention of a garden at the Palace of Falkland was in the time of King Charles I, when the Palace Rolls refer to 'planting and contriving the garden anew'. What the 'contriving' involved is not known, but at the same time the 'yaird dykes' – or outer walls – were practically rebuilt. There is also mention of a sundial and pillar, painted and gilded, these too were destroyed during the occupation of the Palace by Cromwell's soldiers, who also set about the systematic destruction of the magnificent Forest of Falkland.

The loaning, or lonying, beneath the Palace, the site of the present garden, then consisted largely of open grass. In later years it was used as a kitchen garden for the family home nearby, the House of Falkland, and during World War II when labour was scarce and food still scarcer, the whole was put down to potatoes.

Thus, when in 1947 the present Hereditary Keeper, Major Michael Crichton Stuart, made his home at Falkland, only the existing greenhouse remained, surrounded by unkempt yew hedges. The high walls needed to be shored up and everywhere needed repointing. But the ground was clean (the potatoes had seen to that) and it was rich, for, as Jenkin, the then gardener at Falkland, declared, 'the drains of the Palace had been emptying into that spot for centuries'.

It was a daunting prospect that faced Major and Mrs Crichton Stuart, but this was the scene of their remarkable benefaction. There can be few other examples of individuals restoring a garden with their own care, time and money and, when it was nearing completion passing it to the Nation. Yet this is what occurred at Falkland.

The Palace of Falkland is built on a sandstone ridge. The soil is neutral with excellent drainage, and on the whole pleasant to work with. Frost and snow are light problems in this part of Fife, in a normal year; but winds can be a hazard and already the Lawson's cypresses on the upper level of the garden are showing signs of the constant buffeting they receive from the prevailing south-westerly wind, and beginning to lean. Much less friendly are the east winds which blow straight from Saint Andrews and the North Sea, this is a chilling and sometimes killing blow, particularly in the spring.

The first task was to produce another site for the fruit and vegetables then growing on the loaning. These were banished to the site of the present Water Garden, and the yew hedge was extended across the garden, but leaving a gap wide enough to see the Palace. With this done, the true dimensions of the problem before them became apparent. For, from the higher ground, towards which any visitor would normally and naturally gravitate, the loaning stretched like an amphitheatre below. How, therefore, to create a garden which could not all be seen from one point?

Inspiration was found in a seventeenth century engraving which showed a series of island-like clumps of trees, effectively breaking up the open and wide expanse. But how to translate that into gardening parlance? It was here that the Crichton Stuarts came to the conclusion that professional advice was needed, and the commission was given to the distinguished garden architect, Percy Cane.

Cane's solution was to create what has been described as a garden glade, where island beds, planted with trees and tall shrubs provide character and frame vistas in what is otherwise an open space. It was the intention, as Percy Cane describes in his book *The Earth is my Canvas*, to throw into yet higher relief the dominating Palace and to incorporate into the composition the site of the older castle to the north of the existing buildings. To achieve this, he created a series of intermediate levels and planted a number of columnar Lawson's cypresses (*Chamaecyparis lawsoniana*) with the expressed desire of accentuating the height of the ruined wall of the East Range. Yet these also tend to bring the eye down to the loaning below, an effect enhanced by the clever use of paving and flights of stone steps. On the eastern side of the garden along the Palace Dyke, as the great wall there is known, he created the Great Border, fully 180 metres long and six metres wide.

And then, as Cane described to Major Crichton Stuart one day, 'Human nature being what it is, everyone wants to walk *round* a garden, so I've designed a cosy walk right the way round and back to the steps, between the straight edges of the inner beds and outer borders. But up the middle of the garden I've done the opposite, there are no straight edges, there are nothing but curves, to give the full effect of vista and space.'

The six half-moon island beds, which take the place of the isolated clumps of trees in the old engraving, are planted with shrubs and sub-shrubs enjoying the semi-shade beneath laburnums, maples, weigela, philadelphus, a very fine *Fothergilla monticola,* with spikes of white bottle-brush flowers which come out in the spring before the leaves appear, and good autumn colouring; and flowering cherries, including *Prunus yedoensis*, and *Prunus* 'Ukon,' with, curiously, yellow flowers. These beds have the dual role of providing a continuing interest throughout the year, and yet preventing everything being on view at once. Between the beds, alleys and vistas – in effect 'windows' – show the Palace from different angles and also give the impression of the whole arena being very much larger than it in fact is. And in summer the shadows from the taller trees, now nearing maturity, give an altogether appealing sense of peace.

The visitor will first pass through the Reception Centre at the southern end of the garden. Designed to cater for the needs of over

50,000 visitors who come to Falkland during what is effectually a six-month season, it is in the shape of an old weaver's house and was created for the National Trust by Scotland's architect, Schomberg Scott. The Centre has the added advantage of providing some protection from the south-west wind which whistles down the main street of the old town and over the garden wall.

Beyond the Reception Centre is a paved area on two levels. Here a distinguished-looking owl dominates proceedings and an enormous stone draughts-board. To the right leading to the garden proper is the first of Falkland's borders, largely a foliage effect of hostas, libertias, the invaluable yellow-green flowered *Alchemilla mollis*, bergenias and others, set off by two striped grasses *Dactylis glomerata* Variegata and *Alopecurus pratensis* 'Foliis Variegatis' (*Aureus*). This leads to a sundial, also by Schomberg Scott.

From here the visitor can see the Great Border in all its magnificence – but most probably his view will be arrested by four huge rose bushes, trees really, of 'Fruhlingsgold' and 'Fruhlingsmorgen', the tallest nearly 6m. high and broad in proportion.

Whereas, in the early days of the garden, some shrubs pined and others took time to become established, these four throve, almost indecently, and for no reason that anyone could fathom. It remained a mystery until, one winter's morning, with the frost white on the ground, it was noticed that a line of unfrozen earth ran diagonally across the top corner of the garden and under the roses. Investigation ensued and it was then remembered that there was a drain which carried the waste from the linoleum factory above the town. Thus for years the roses had been enjoying the bottom heat of hot linseed oil, and thriving on it. The linoleum factory has long since closed, the flow of linseed oil is no more, but the roses given this unusual start to life continue to thrive and in June each year the cascade of bloom from these four is one of the sights of Falkland.

In this setting, 180 metres of unrelieved herbaceous border, however cleverly planted, would have been overwhelming, so shrubs and trees have been included at either end. The transition from shrub to herbaceous plant is gradual and the lower centre of the Great Border brings out the greater height of the island beds. A flowering progression runs down the border with the main block of bright colours – reds, yellows and oranges – in the centre and at their best in July to September – the height of the tourist season.

The effect is stunning, yet so well has the balance been maintained between the broad sweep of colour on the one hand and the majesty of the ancient Palace on the other that the whole seems in perfect harmony.

Behind this magnificent border the walls are clothed with climbers and wall shrubs of all sorts: *Escallonia* 'Apple Blossom', a great favourite; clematis in profusion, and roses, amongst others the ever-popular 'Albertine', the early-flowering flame-pink 'Madame Edouard Herriot', *Rosa gigantea,* a species from Burma and an old rambler 'Amethyste', whose rich violet flowers in huge clusters are sensational in July.

At the north end of the Great Border are two enormous stone pots with a planting of *Gentiana sino-ornata* and *Vitis coignetiae,* a most effective combination. These guard the entrance to the newly-built water-garden. Designed around two raised rectangular water basins with a planting motif of low-growing junipers – *Juniperus communis* 'Hornibrookii' and *J. horizontalis* – with four Pencil Cedars (*Juniperus virginiana*) to add distinction, this is a garden in complete contrast to the profusion and glorious colours of the Great Border. It creates a fitting prelude to the approach to the old Tennis Court.

It is between the two guardian stone pots that the best view of the Palace and its loaning may be obtained. From here the full grandeur of the scene and the genius of the planting and design by Percy Cane and the Crichton Stuarts can be properly appreciated. Dominating everything in high summer is the white lattice of an enormous Russian Vine, *Polygonum baldschuanicum* which smothers a buttress of the old East Range. Below, the neutral colours of greys and whites, and light blues – from *Romneya coulteri,* growing on what must be the draughtiest corner of the garden and evidently liking it; *Aster frikartii,* hostas, the grey-leaved *Artemisia absinthum,* delphiniums and *Salvia* × *superba*. This is a very cleverly associated border.

On the upper level beyond the sentinel Lawson's is a formal rose garden picked out in the livery colours of the Stewarts – provided by Floribunda roses, the red 'Frensham' and the yellow 'Allgold', surrounded by hard-clipped 'tables' of grey *Senecio laxifolius,* pyramids of golden yew and lavender.

To the west, towards the new orchard is a small wood, a place of solitude, not noticed and rarely visited. A scene of dappled shade and a path leading to a modern 'shadowe-house' overlooking what used to be a curling pond where the traditional Scottish winter game had been played for as long as anyone could remember – it is now a bowling-green. This is a place of tranquillity, a place to ponder on the turbulent history of Falkland, the genius of the new creation, and the benevolence of those who have held the old Palace in this care for the last one hundred years.

Handed down from generation to generation, the Palace of Falkland is still the property of Her Majesty the Queen. But no sovereign has lived here since the days of King Charles, and care of the Palace has been left with an Hereditary Keeper. Although maintaining the fabric is no part of their charge, many Keepers have done so at their own expense; and much of the restoration has been achieved without recourse to public funds. Chief of these was the 3rd Marquess of Bute who became, to give him his full title, Hereditary Constable, Captain and Keeper of the Palace of Falkland in 1887.

No account of Falkland can be complete without tribute to the 3rd Marquess, one of the most remarkable benefactors these islands have ever seen. Bute, liturgist and linguist, traveller and scholar, in Scotland alone restored the Castle of Rothesay, the Old Place of Mochrum and the Priories of Saint Andrews and Pluscarden in Moray. Following the start made by his father, he largely created the City of Cardiff as we know it today, he even turned his hand to growing vines in South Wales, with mixed success. A man of immense energy with a wide range of accomplishments, he it was who excavated the old castle of Falkland and the burned down North Range. He also completely restored the South Range which stands today and was setting out to do the same to the East Range, when he died.

The process of modernising the South Range and restoring the Palace Precinct was carried on by the present Keeper when he came to live at Falkland after the war. But the burden of such a charge is considerable, so it came about that, in 1952, Major Crichton Stuart ensured the safe-keeping and preservation of the Royal Palace of Falkland 'in all time coming', by appointing the National Trust for Scotland to be his Deputy Keeper. This was achieved by the grant of an historic charter, along with a substantial endowment.

Royal visits to Falkland are rare – in fact from 1650 to 1820 there were none – but happily they are now more frequent, and in 1958, the Queen was able to be present at the 500th anniversary of the granting of the Charter to the ancient Royal Burgh of Falkland.

Once again the old red walls of the Palace of Falkland gazed down upon masque and merriment. The ghosts of Whistle-Gibbon, Bell-the-Cat, the Wild Lady and the blind Poet Harry and the many other characters who had passed across the stage of 500 years of Stewart history walked again. And few who attended that last Royal occasion cannot but have been moved by the atmosphere and mellow tranquillity of the old Palace which has seen so much of Scotland's history.

How to get there

18 km north of KIRKCALDY; 6 km south of AUCHTERMUCHTY; 60 km EDINBURGH
A92 north from KIRKCALDY – fork left at MUIRHEAD on *A912*
A91 off EDINBURGH-PERTH Motorway (M90) turn right on to *A912* at STRATHMIGLO

TWO

Pitmedden *Aberdeenshire*
Edzell *Angus*

A GARDEN IS a living entity: unless it can grow, can change and can develop it will decline and may disappear forever. So it has sadly been with the seventeenth century Parterre garden in this country – a garden style characterised by great charm and individuality. For the ravages of time and neglect, and the heavy hand of the 'Improvers' of the eighteenth-century Landscape School have swept away all but a distressingly few examples. But Scotland is fortunate in possessing two of the finest survivors, gardens of great appeal and fascination. They have been reconstructed, it is true, but reconstructed as far as can be determined along the lines of the original designs. These are Edzell Castle in Angus, owned by the Department of the Environment, and the much larger property of the National Trust for Scotland at Pitmedden in Aberdeenshire.

The Scotland of the sixteenth and early seventeenth centuries was a bleak country. Travellers of the period invariably comment on the sparsity of growth, for there were few trees or bushes except for the occasional clump around castle or manse; instead there prevailed a barren, cold, uninviting landscape as inhospitable as the inns which were renowned for their discomfort and nastiness.

The style of architecture was the castellated building of turret and battlement, or the austere two-storied dwelling houses with their distinctive corbel-stepped gable roofs. The sites for the houses were chosen more for the need for defence against attack than with any aesthetic value in mind, and there was no love for the indigenous scenery.

Husbandry was primitive in the extreme and knowledge of draining almost unknown. Crop rotation had not been discovered and run-rig* cultivation the normal, and highly uneconomic fashion. Hedges – the plants often imported from Holland – were a strongly opposed rarity for they were believed to draw strength from the soil as well as harbour the birds which devoured the crops. What enclosures there were could be found around the houses, so the few miserable cattle anyone owned roamed at will over the largely unenclosed countryside. The only vegetable known was colewort or kail – a type of Greens – and the primitive huts were of stone with roofs of turves and often no chimneys. Even if the countryfolk had the inclination to improve their properties, they were hamstrung by the system of land tenure which was for short leases at the whim of their landlord.

The better-off found little time, or inclination for the finer things of life, and in general their gardens were strictly utilitarian. Yet gardens there were, particularly in the more congenial climate of the Lothians around Edinburgh, which was 'beautified with fair orchards and gardens' by at least the middle of the sixteenth century.

Two features dominated the evolution of the Scottish garden of this period; the domestic and political instability of the country which slowed the application of new ideas; and, the delusion almost amounting to confirmed prejudice – and a ready excuse – that few plants could survive a Scottish winter. It was Dr Johnson who was said to have pronounced that the Scottish climate was such that barley could only be grown under glass. Even trees – the oak, the sycamore and the chestnut – were considered tender, and they were clustered around house or manse as much for their own protection from the elements. Not until after the Union with England in 1707 did tree planting become commonplace, and the misconception of the hardiness of some plants in the rigour of a Scottish winter persisted until well into the nineteenth century.

As in England, it was the later 1600s, after the Restoration of Charles II, that was to see a noticeable transformation in garden

---

* *RUN-RIG*
In run-rig cultivation the fields were subdivided into long, narrow strips so that any particularly productive land could not be monopolised by one tenant. The division was achieved by forming ridges some three to four metres across, separated by shallow gulleys – into which grain and seeds were inevitably washed. Such a system was extremely wasteful of land, yet in parts of Scotland it persisted until the nineteenth century, and many traces can be seen today.

design in Scotland. But, as in any change in taste, general acceptance and assimilation was a slow process; Scotland was many years behind comparable movements in England and France.

In Scotland a greater stability, a relief from the almost continual turmoil which had stalked the country for so long, made men begin to want, and to realise, the ease and comfort they had observed and experienced elsewhere. The style of domestic architecture started to broaden, manor houses came to be built in place of the castles of old, and sites were now increasingly chosen for their inherently pleasing outlook and situation. The Pleasure Garden, the 'Great Garden' as it was known, became an architectural extension to the house, and garden design came to assume as great a significance as design of the house itself.

The intricate, strictly symmetrical Knot Garden of Elizabethan England was one of small compartments. Each compartment was, according to contemporary horticulturists, to be a foot or so above the level of the path, of such a size that 'the weeders handes may well reach into the middest of the bed' and the level was to 'be kept to a haire, for if you faill in it you faill in your whole work'. The word knot passed from common usage in the reign of Charles – the parterre, a more elaborate piece of work, but otherwise very similar, took its place. Still essentially geometrical, the parterre was less fussy and on a larger scale; it was designed to be seen from above, often as the foreground to an extensive formal landscape, and relied on immediate impact for effect. How well this last has been achieved by the recreators of the Great Garden of Pitmedden.

Parterre design varied from the merely picturesque to the patently absurd. Those in France, in particular, were symptomatic of the lavishness and ornateness of the Grand Siècle, for the simpler, more effective and more dignified older geometric pattern had given way to designs which bordered on the fantastic.

In Tudor times, the edgings of knots had been of rosemary, lavender, thyme, hyssop, rue, thrift, juniper or box – but by now the box was in almost universal use. The range of plants by modern standards was meagre, but the indigenous and European plants formerly employed had been vastly extended by foreign importations, the 'outlandish' plants, they were called. Already the activities of plant hunters were beginning to show fruit, and none more prolific that John Tradescant the Elder, a 'Painful industrious searcher and lover of all Nature's varieties'.

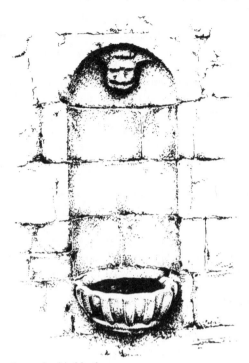

Pitmedden: a decorative bird bath.

The name of Seton holds an honoured place in the annals of Scotland. An ancient and noble House, for many centuries the Setons made their mark on Scottish affairs and were noted 'even in feudal times for the more graceful and civilising tendencies of the age', as the family historian describes. Granted estates in the eleventh century, the Setons acquired properties and power over the succeeding years by judicious purchases of land, and a no less astute choice of brides. The Seton interest in land was evidently of long-standing, for as early as the beginning of the sixteenth century, the then Lord Seton possessed a garden and orchards which were reputed to be the fairest in all Scotland. It was clearly a remarkable confection, the flower beds surrounded by little wooden temples each with its chime of gilded bells – all were destroyed by English troops in 1564. Elsewhere, the Setons had been prominent in promoting careful, sensible husbandry.

In 1603, one James Seton of Bourtie acquired the property of

Pitmedden near the village of Udny in Aberdeenshire, and became its first Laird. But it was Alexander Seton, son of the third Laird, who was creator of what has become known as the Great Garden of Pitmedden.

While the boy was still young, the third Laird was killed bearing King Charles I's Standard at the Battle of the Brig O'Dee, so the young Setons, Alexander and his elder brother James, were taken as wards by their kinsman the Earl of Winton. With him they lived in a world far removed from the rustic regime they had enjoyed in the wilds of Aberdeenshire, where many castles and fortified dwellings still bear witness to the insecurity and backwardness of the region at that time. Winton was a man of culture, possessing great wealth, a fine library and a wide circle of friends; thus his tutelage was far-ranging.

In 1667, however, James was killed in battle, and Alexander fell heir to the Pitmedden estate. Sir Alexander Seton – he had been knighted by Charles II in 1664 – was then an Advocate and divided his time between Edinburgh and Pitmedden. On 2 May 1675, as the carving above the doorway which to this day serves as entrance to the garden testifies, Alexander and his wife, Dame Margaret Lauder, founded the Great Garden of Pitmedden.

A fire in 1818 destroyed the family papers and portraits as well as severely damaging the fabric of the old house, so we have no certain knowledge of the original design of the Great Garden. But this was a period of much gardening activity, in England and France as well as in Scotland. It is likely that Sir Alexander Seton had read the works of the Mollet family, of John Evelyn and other horticultural writers. A more probable source of inspiration was Sir William Bruce then engaged on the rebuilding of the Palace of Holyroodhouse.

Bruce, close confidant and friend of Charles II for many years, had made several journeys to France, and it was during these that he met and became influenced by the work of André Le Nôtre, then engaged on his masterpiece at Versailles. In 1671, Bruce was given the sonorous title of 'The King's Surveyor and Master of Works', and set about the restoration of Holyrood which had been allowed to fall into disrepair. At the same time John Rose, Charles II's own gardener, drew up plans and set all in motion for the creation of the formal garden at the Palace no vestige of the old garden remains today, but from engravings in a folio entitled *A Bird's Eye View of Edinburgh* it is possible to see how it must have looked. It was from

1 *top* Falkland Palace. The formal paving

2 *above* Edzell. Note the niches in the wall at the back

3 Pitmedden. The Grand Parterre

this drawing that the design of the reconstructed parterres at Pitmedden was based.

Another source, nearer at hand and on the road from Edinburgh, was the formal garden at Edzell Castle. Created by Sir David Lindsay, Lord Edzell, scion of a House – the 'Lichtsome Lindsays' – as old and no less noble than that of Seton and to whom the Setons were distantly connected, the garden at Edzell, though less well known and constructed on a much smaller scale than that at Pitmedden, possesses a unique charm.

The site at Edzell is vastly different from that at Pitmedden. Situated in a hollow at the junction of two rivers, Edzell was primarily a fortress. Any concession to comfort or beauty came later, an adjunct to the principal purpose of the castle. Even the walls, which are such a feature of the garden, were constructed with half a mind to defensive needs and still show the original embrasures. This preoccupation with defence meant that the whole garden had to be constructed within the constrained space bounded by the old moat – although this was swept away in a flood in the middle of the eighteenth century. Thus it is that the formal garden at Edzell is only some sixty paces square. But within this small area is possibly the oldest complete garden design in Britain, and certainly one of the greatest charm.

A contemporary writer noted: 'The Castle or Palace of Edzell is an excellent dwelling, a great house, delicate garden, with walls sumptuously built of hewn stone, polished, with pictures and coats of arms in the walls . . . .' The pictures and coats of arms as well as the statues have long since vanished, but what remains of the walls themselves is remarkable enough.

The architect of the magnificent and unique walls is not known. But Sir David Lindsay was a man of culture and taste, who travelled widely, and there is a strong Italian presence about some of the carving. Some of the panels were evidently taken from a sixteenth-century book of German engravings, and copied by local craftsmen of varied skill and education, for even the initials of the engraver have been studiously carved.

Under Sir David Lindsay, who was a man of parts, Edzell became prominent in the district and, evidently, possessed a tree nursery, one of the earliest in Scotland. Not least renowned for its table, it was known as the 'Kitchen of Angus', largely, we must believe because of the 'Guid kuik', one Edward Stevens, an Englishman and evidently versatile as he is recorded, with some awe, as being adept at making 'baked meats' and the 'Inglish planting of hedges'.

Although the site at Pitmedden is six times the size of the garden at Edzell, nevertheless it did not permit the lavishness which was the hallmark of the great formal gardens of the age. Despite this, the formal Great Garden of Pitmedden was no small achievement. Sir Alexander Seton – he was further honoured in 1677 and created Lord Pitmedden – first levelled and shaped the ground which today forms the upper garden. To the east, the soil was excavated and a sunken garden made, a hectare in extent; around this, high retaining walls of granite were constucted on all four sides. In keeping with the idea that parterre gardens should be seen from above, a terrace was raised above the main garden. And, again with a traditional flavour, each end of the medial wall was concluded with a two-storied pavilion; these are now surmounted by weather-vanes in the form of the Seton crest. The north pavilion is of particular interest; the upper chamber was evidently panelled in oak and apparently served as a summer house; the lower apartment had a fireplace and a small cubicle for storing fuel – and could have been used as a bath house.

The main access to the lower garden was in the centre of the north wall. Here, two stone pillars marked the entrance to a formal twin flight of stone steps which descended to the parterres below. One of the earliest of writers on Scottish gardens was John Reid who wrote in his *The Scots Gard'ner,* published in 1683, eight years after Sir Alexander started his great work that, 'Pleasure grounds should be divided into plots by walls, with "Bordures" round each plot, and an evergreen trimmed in pyramidal fashion at each corner'. This is the broad concept that the National Trust for Scotland has adopted at Pitmedden.

In its heyday, the Great Garden of Pitmedden must have been a wonderful sight – although, surprisingly, there is no mention of it by travellers. The sole reference is in a statistical account early in the last century. This records that at Pitmedden was 'one of the finest and best laid out gardens in the north of Scotland', which, 'produces apples and pears especially the former, superior to any in Scotland'. But thereafter it steadily declined.

In 1894 the Pitmedden Estate came up for sale and was bought by Alexander Keith, and it remained in that family's hands until James

Keith, the last Laird of Pitmedden, bequeathed the property to the National Trust for Scotland, in 1953. Thus the Trust fell heir to what was that little more than a shell, but was potentially one of the most important sites in Scottish Gardening history.

The late Dr James S. Richardson, one time Inspector of Ancient Monuments in Scotland, had been instrumental in recreating the formal garden at Edzell, so this new task was entrusted to his care. In 1956 work commenced. As no record remained of the designs of the former parterres – any record there may have been having been burnt in the fire of 1818 – inspiration was found in the book of folio engravings published in 1647, referred to earlier, for three of the quarters, and the fourth, as tribute to Lord Pitmedden, took the form of his coat of arms.

To start with, it was necessary to grass down the whole area, and then to mark out the designs and plant a boxwood outline. First to be created was the Seton coat of arms, a task requiring no less than three kilometres-worth of box-plants, at the same time, the existing English yews were planted. From the experience so gained it was possible to continue the main outlines in subsequent years, and in 1958 took place the first planting of herbaceous plants within the parterres.

To provide extra emphasis and to highlight the intricacies of the designs, two great borders were drawn up by Lady Burnett of Leys, the creator of Crathes Garden, another horticultural gem in this part of Scotland. These borders must be seen from above, so great blocks of colour are needed and an extended flowering season is required. This effect has been provided by monkshood and campanula, alstromeria and sidalcea, golden rod and achillea. At the front of the border are geraniums and *Orchis maderensis,* kniphofias, phlox and antholyza.

On the walls behind are fan-trained plums and espalier-trained apples. On the northern side, great buttresses of yew have been grown, the entrances alternatively open or closed with a low hedge of variegated box, behind which are Floribunda roses with clematis and honeysuckle growing on the walls. In one corner by the stone steps may be found a good plant of *Crinodendron hookerianum,* on the west wall a number of *Vitis coignetiae* and the Cape Figwort, *Phygelius capensis.* But this is no plantsman's garden; it is designed to create impact from afar, and that it certainly does.

During the excavations it was discovered that originally there had been two burn-fed water outlets into the garden. The one on the upper terrace, where it is known that Sir Alexander had constructed a fountain has now been repeated and a lily pond built round the new fountain, using fragments of stone found on the site, including a piece with four mask heads, which may well have come from the original fountain. The whole is placed in a formal setting of pleached limes, and centred on two venerable yews, which are believed to be at least 200 years old.

The central focal point of the lower level is another fountain, surrounded by a pavement of split pebbles – an effective paving, if a remarkably uncomfortable one. Several of the sculptured stones which comprise this second fountain are of great antiquity and once formed part of the Cross Fountain of Linlithgow in West Lothian. These are known to have been designed and executed by Robert Milne, Master Mason to Charles II.

Another feature, worthy of notice, is the sundial in the south-east parterre. This magnificent stone has twenty-four facets and dates from the seventeenth century. As it was found in the garden, it is reasonable to suppose that it must have been incorporated in the original design. Another may be found on the wall of the North Pavilion.

Since 1956 the garden has gradually matured. The plum and apple trees are now fully grown, the *Rosa rubrifolia,* which looks so effective against a vast yew in the north-east corner of the garden, has now climbed six metres high into its host. The yews, which flank the main allée, are now fine symmetrical specimens, and the dwarf box has thickened to provide the clear outlines and patterns which make the parterre garden.

Each year some 30,000 annual plants are used to give colour to the designs. Experience and experiment has revealed the most consistent varieties, those which reach their peak at the same time and are reliable in the vagaries of the East Aberdeenshire weather – for Pitmedden is only 13 kilometres from the coast and the climate here can prove tricky, especially with evergreens. The popular choice nowadays to fill the parterre beds are alyssum, begonias and dwarf wallflowers, while extensive use is made of grey gravel to provide a touch of contrast. The effect is striking, particularly from afar, but the muted elegance of, say, the *potagers* at Villandry is missing – or of the delight that once met the eyes of Sir Alexander Seton's guests so many years ago, when none of these gaudy plants existed and the gardeners of the day must rely on the soft tones of rue and hyssop, rosemary or thrift, interspersed with coloured earths or stones.

'C'est magnifique', as a visitor was heard to exclaim, 'mais ce n'est pas un jardin.' That is too harsh a judgement on a wonderful gardening achievement. But, perhaps, he has a point.

How to get there

EDZELL
10 km north of BRECHIN
A94 north from BRECHIN – after 4 km fork left on to *B966*

PITMEDDEN
23 km north of ABERDEEN; 2 km north of UDNY
A92 north from ABERDEEN – then *B999* 6 km north of ABERDEEN

THREE

Culzean *Ayrshire*

JOURNEYING NORTH along the coast road, some 12 kilometres beyond the little harbour of Girvan, past the early-potato fields of Ayrshire and the golf-course at Turnberry, a great tree-clad bluff can be seen overlooking the sea. This is the site of Culzean (pronounced Cul-lane) whose Castle and Country Park annually attract over a quarter of a million visitors.

Dominating the eastern approach to the Firth of Clyde, the strategic importance of this position is immediately clear. For centuries, Culzean has been a fortified site, inaccessible from the sea, where steep cliffs sweep unhindered to the rocks below and where there are caves approachable only at low tide. Formerly, an arm of the Firth all but cut off the rock on which the castle stands, making the stronghold a virtual island approached only by a causeway on the site of the present roadway, and a narrow land bridge on the Green to the west of the Castle.

This immensely strong castle was one of the homes of the Kennedys, and a part of the chain of fortresses built to protect the vulnerable, rich inland areas of Ayrshire. Invasions of Vikings and fellow-Scots, the Highland chieftains – no less rapacious than those plunderers from further afield – were a common threat. The most recent scare was from Napoleon, when the then Laird of Culzean raised a regiment and had gun emplacements built to resist the promised invasion.

Vast landowners – the Kennedys possessed over forty estates in their heyday – powerful, turbulent and liable to find offence in the slightest act that displeased them, they ruled the southern part of Ayrshire, known as Carrick, in unpredictable sway for five centuries.

Twixt Wigton and the town of Ayr,
Portpatrick and the Cruives of Cree,
No man needs think for to bide there,
Unless he court with Kennedie.

runs an old rhyme.

When not fighting their neighbours, they would fight to the death among themselves. The most noteworthy of their doings, which even revolted their contèmporaries, hardened as they were to the cruelty and suffering of the age, was the act known as the Roasting of the Abbot of Crossraguel – in the Black Vault of the Castle of Dunure, another Kennedy stronghold some ten kilometres north of Culzean. He, poor man, was cooked twice over a slow fire for refusing to surrender his Abbey lands to a Kennedy who coveted them.

From time to time peace reigned insecurely between the rival factions of the family but soon, it would be broken in bloody conflict once again. On one occasion of truce it was decided to cement the passing friendship with marriage between two of the principal branches of the clan. All was arranged; a piper approached Culzean up the long western approach to the castle to set the ceremony in

Culzean: Fountain Court.

motion. The skirl of the pipes could be heard in the distance by the waiting wedding guests. Gradually it was getting nearer – then, silence, the piper had vanished and was never heard of more. But he gave his name to the path he had been walking – the Piper's Brae.

The sixteenth century saw the Kennedys at the zenith of their power, but thereafter the great family began to decline in prestige and influence. The Kennedy of the time had been created Earl of Cassilis in 1509, but it was the 9th, and to a greater extent the 10th Earls, both of whom died as bachelors, that the Castle, gardens and estate of Culzean as we know it today are due.

The eighteenth century, and particularly the latter half of it, was the age of the great 'Improvers' in Scottish agriculture and general husbandry. A succession of Land Acts during the last years of the previous century had set about the long-overdue reform of the land-tenure system in Scotland – the demise of the old, uneconomic run-rig farming was now inevitable. This was just the impetus needed; another came from the Act of Union with England in 1707. Soon the closer commercial ties with the more advanced agricultural system south of the Border began to show benefit in Scotland. A more equable and economic system of landowner and tenant farmer arose, this in turn led to better farming methods. Significantly, in 1723, the first Agricultural Society was formed, which provided the general spur that had been lacking. Large, fenced fields, shelter belts and woodlands, drainage, manuring and crop rotations took the place of the previous primitive cultivation. In addition 'The Honourable the Society of Improvers in the Knowledge of Agriculture in Scotland', was instrumental in spreading the popularity of the turnip, and probably helped to advertise the merits of the potato, which had first been grown in Scotland in 1725, but which was not generally accepted for another fifty years.

With the general increase shown in husbandry, the gardens were not neglected. As with agriculture, gradually the influence from south of the Border began to percolate into Scottish gardens. This was the age culminating in the Landscape School in England, the age of Switzer, Bridgeman, Kent, and above all Lancelot (Capability) Brown. Stephen Switzer enjoyed a prolonged stay around 1717 and was responsible for a number of estates and gardens around Edinburgh – among them Newliston, Hopetoun and Dalkeith House, and Brown is known to have spent a while in

Scotland. But the new gardening philosophy found little general favour north of the Border, and well into the eighteenth century the formal garden continued to survive, even to be built in Scotland. Thus when the subsequent craze for Victorian planting in geometrical beds in seried ranks reached Scotland, a ready framework was to hand. But the landscape style was not wholly neglected. One of the first landscape gardens in Scotland was made by Lord Kames at Blair Drummond, but its landscape element more nearly corresponded to the 'Wild Garden' of a later age.

Not until the Landscape School was on the decline in England was a real impact made on the Scottish gardening scene, and it was a disastrous one. For at the indifferent hands of the journeyman landscape gardener, the charm and seclusion of all too many Scottish gardens was erased from everything but memory – particularly in the Border counties. An outspoken opponent of the new, plagiarised school was that most famous of Scotsmen, Sir Walter Scott, who thundered against the movement. Writing of a much-loved garden he had once known he complained of the hedges cut down 'the trees stubbed up, and the whole character of the place so much destroyed that we were glad when we could leave it.' And of Duddingstone, a house near Edinburgh, where extensive work had been carried out by one Robertson, a pupil of Brown, and who had created a series of ponds and water-falls, these he likened to a string of pork-sausages! Under this, and other attacks, the Landscape School found little general acceptance.

A foremost 'Improver' in the area around Ayr was the 9th Earl of Cassilis. He seems to have been a far-sighted and benevolent landlord, and the parish minister could write of the early 1770s at Culzean that 'the husbandry of the parish underwent a total and happy revolution'. The 9th Earl died in 1775, to be succeeded by his brother, and he it was who commissioned Robert Adam to refashion the old Castle of Culzean.

1777 is given as the date of the start of the work at Culzean (really the site of what used to be known as the Castle of Coiff – the true Culzean has never been found, but is believed to have been on the site of the kitchen-garden). For thirteen years thereafter there was to be almost continuous building operations in train. First the original keep, or Peel Tower, was incorporated; then the great Drum Tower was built hanging on the very lip of the cliff over-looking the Firth, and with an unrivalled view across the water to Ailsa Craig and the mountains of the Isle of Arran; finally, Adam's magnificent oval domed staircase – the pride of Culzean – was added to unite the two halves of the Castle.

Not neglected were the policies – as in Scotland the garden and immediate surroundings of a house are called; for the Stable Block, with a central clock tower, was built by Adam, as was the Home Farm which is now the Park Centre. This, a design of the greatest charm, and highly functional, was long considered to be one of Culzean's chief attractions. But it was in poor repair, the old red sandstone in places disintegrating, so it was decided to restore the whole and convert the barns and outbuildings into a restaurant, shop and exhibition wing. Work was started in 1971, similar coloured stone was brought from as far afield as Northumberland and Durham and the whole was brought to triumphal completion in 1975, in time to win an Award of Outstanding Architectural Merit for European Heritage Year.

Adam also built the present bridge to the Castle on the site of the old causeway, and constructed the arch, purposely 'ruined' in the style of the time. It is also believed that he redesigned the terraces and Fountain Court below the Castle.

Years earlier, the inlet of the sea, which had been Culzean's chief defence from the landward side for centuries, had been filled in to create a glen – a completely protected place where a local minister in 1693 could describe 'these gardens as being so well sheltered from the North and East winds and ly so open to the South that the fruits and herbage are more early than any other place in Carrict'. He comments too on the 'very pretty gardens and orchards, adorned with excellent terrasses', laden with peaches, apricots, cherries and other fruit. For the Gulf Stream provides a gentle and equable climate, where there is protection from the wind. The rainfall is high – in excess of 150 cm. – but not as high as some other places on the west coast of Scotland. Frost and snow occur, but rarely linger. The soil is a light, sandy loam with excellent drainage.

It is nearly certain that the 'terrasses' were altered by Adam to their present form, but who saw to the laying out of the garden is more obscure. It is believed that two men, Robinson and Whyte, possibly pupils of Brown, were responsible, but it is also thought that Alexander Nasmyth, the eminent Scottish portrait and landscape painter, who also numbered landscape design among his considerable talents, may have had a hand in shaping the layout of the outer policies. Be that as it may, by the turn of the nineteenth century, another minister can report that 'on the land side and immediately below the castle are the gardens belonging to the old house of Cullean, formed out of rock at great expense into three terraces; upon the walls of which are planted some of the choicest fruit trees. The remainder of the old garden is formed into pleasure grounds and gravel walks kept with great care.' And the Walled Garden, possibly also influenced by Nasmyth, dates from 1783. A Day Book, which covers the period from 1780 to the second decade of the next century, shows the care and attention the 10th Earl paid to his husbandry. In this there is mention of load after load of earth and 'moss' – presumably peat moss – being brought from outside to provide substance and to mix with the light sandy loam of the kitchen garden. We get a fascinating insight into the enquiring and questing mind of one of the great 'Improvers' in such notes as 'How long will it take 20 beasts to manure four acres?' There is too meticulous mention of the thousand upon thousand trees ordered and planted and kept clean – this last a job for the 'older men'!

The 12th Earl was an intimate of the Duke of Clarence. When the latter came to the throne as King William IV, he created his long-standing friend 1st Marquess of Ailsa in 1831. It is largely he, and his great-grandson the 3rd Marquess, who were responsible for the final shaping of Culzean. It was the 1st Marquess who started the planting of the many 'exotics' which graced the terrace walls, some of which still survive. He it was who constructed the Orangery at the further end of the Fountain Court. A common enough feature in the gardens of great houses south of the Border, the orangery never excited the same enthusiasm in Scotland. Of all the house plants so beloved by our Victorian ancestors the orange trees – sometimes reaching colossal proportions and requiring complicated equipment to enable them to be moved at all – were the most treasured. They were grown chiefly for the beautifully-scented orange blossom borne more or less continuously throughout the year.

And so the garden at Culzean gradually came to assume its present design, and it is not difficult to imagine how it must have looked when it was at its glorious best in the years before the First World War.

The first feature the visitor will notice after his arrival, will be the ruined Adam arch at the end of the bridge spanning what is now the

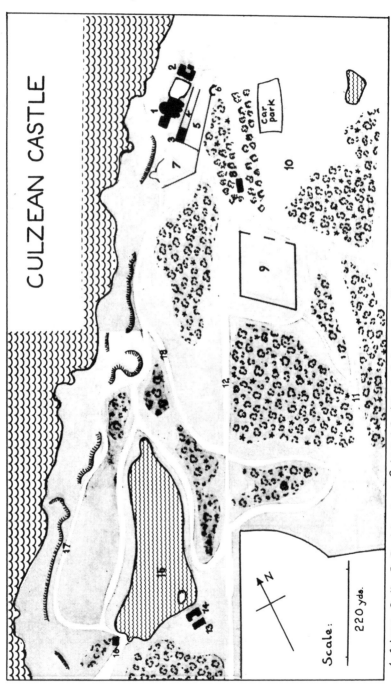

CULZEAN CASTLE

car park

Scale:

220 yds.

N

1. Culzean Castle 5. Fountain Court 9. Walled Garden 13. Aviary   17. Cliff Path
2. Clock Tower   6. Ruined Arch   10. Deer Park   14. Swan Cottage 18. Laundry Maid's Walk

glen, its battlemented parapet too designed by Adam to conform with the general appearance of the Castle. To the left and below is stretched the Fountain Court, dominated by the huge, ornate Victorian fountain. On the bank opposite the Castle are the smooth slopes of a heather and shrub border designed to give colour and contour throughout the year. Apart from an extensive planting of ericas, here too are yuccas, bamboos, *Viburnum plicatum* 'Mariesii', escallonias and *Olearia macrodonta,* one of the New Zealand Daisy Bushes whose great, grey holly-like leaves are a common sight at Culzean, where this highly accommodating shrub does exceptionally well.

On the opposite side, under the Castle and the 'terrasses', a line of the Cabbage Palm (*Cordyline australis*) gives an appropriately tropical air to the confection that is Culzean. Behind these palms and flanked on one side by the Orangery and some shrub beds planted to give a continuing interest, are the famous terraces, home of many an exciting plant. Two olearas invariably cause comment, *O. phlogopappa* (*gunniana*) with narrow oblong grey-green leaves and white felted undersides. This has 2cm white daisy flowers. There is also a pink variety in the border as well as *O. paniculata* (*forsteri*) a rare shrub with the bright olive-green wavy leaves of a *Pittosporum tenuifolium,* with which it is sometimes confused. *Feijoa sellowiana* from Mexico with grey leaves and fleshy crimson and white flowers is another unusual shrub – both flowers and the berries which follow are edible. Others include *Solanum crispum* with its conspicuous potato-flowers in late summer, mimosa, roses, clematis, and callistemon, the Australian Bottle-Brush. *Leptospermum lanigerum* (*pubescens*), a member of the myrtle family with long silvery leaves which bronze nicely in the autumn, is another particularly desirable plant. It has white flowers a little over 1cm across in June and July.

Having seen the Fountain Court and Orangery it is best to retrace one's steps, and, after recrossing the glen bridge, to strike off to the right into a woodland path, cool and sheltered. Here one is walking beneath some of Culzean's most glorious trees, particularly the great Silver Firs (*Abies alba*) which were planted in the 1850s. Magnificent giants, but the salt air is beginning to affect the tops of some and they must then be topped to prevent branches falling. And there are other trees of note: a *Sciadopitys verticillata,* the Japanese Umbrella Pine – so-called from the shape of the long bright-green needles which radiate like the spokes of the umbrella – a slow-growing tree with attractive reddish bark; a Mexican Pine (*Pinus montezumae*) with 25cm. needles, a very conspicuous tree, grows nearby; across the road is a Monterey Cypress (*Cupressus macrocarpa*).

The path takes one straight to the Camellia House, another creation of the 2nd Marquess, the design having been taken from a similar one in the family's home in Richmond Park in London. In this area too are a number of unusual plants enjoying the complete seclusion and balmy climate, including *Azara serrata,* whose scented yellow flower clusters stand out wonderfully against the dark-green crenulated leaves; *Crinodendron hookerianum,* a native of Chile with beautiful crimson lantern-shaped flowers hanging from the branches, and a curious rubus with 10cm. long, deeply-serrated petals giving it the appearance of a monstrous insect. Below the Camellia House are four sentinel *Magnolia* x *soulangiana* and on either side a planting of camellias. Another plant that should not be missed is an unusual variant of the common laburnum, with longer pale yellow racemes and leaves conspicuously bundled in whorls along the branches, this is *Laburnum anagyroides* 'Involutum'.

Ahead is the walled-garden, as is so often the case in Scottish, and Irish houses a distance from the main building. Why this is so has never been properly determined. In some cases, as here, the siting was a case of sheer necessity as there is no other reasonably flat spot suitably near at hand. In others, the original position of the house was chosen for exclusively defensive needs, once again a suitable site for a walled-garden might then be a good way away. But in a number of instances these reasons do not hold good and others must be sought. It might be that when the walled-garden was built to site it near the house would obtrude on a landscape scheme, and so it was banished to distant parts. Or perhaps, as John Reid one of the earliest of Scots gardening authors who wrote *The Scots Gard'ner* in 1683, said it was 'because of the impropriety of the view to see manure in that garden when the persons in the house should be more agreeably entertained'.

The Walled Garden at Culzean is unusual in that there is a long wall down the middle, dividing the area into two roughly equal parts. The upper side used to be devoted to fruit and vegetables for the house. Against the walls, in what are now tool and equipment sheds, were the bothies for the gardeners to live in. Some fruit and vegetables still grow here, but there are also two wide herbaceous borders down the centre of this large expanse.

The lower half, sheltered by great six-metre high stone walls, is devoted to grass, rose beds and specimen trees. To the right is the old peach house and beyond are a number of raised stone beds which take the eye to what is known as the Chinese House, a charming thatched summer house where the family frequently used to have their tea in days gone by. Beyond that is a grotto, another Victorian feature. Whether this one ever held a hermit as was customary, is not known (or even, when hermits were in short supply and considered too pricy, if a stuffed one was placed there – as indeed did happen), but the grotto at Culzean creates a perfect setting for a cascade of African Daisy, *Dimorphotheca (Osteospermum) barbariae* and the not very well-known relation of the hebe, *Parahebe catarractae*, whose eyebright flowers are such a useful addition to any sunny or half-shady spot in June and July.

On the left, are a number of rose beds holding shrub and species roses. Beyond and behind a screen of cedar and a very large *Cryptomeria japonica* is a grove of Cabbage Palms and a number of specimen trees: *Catalpa bignonioides,* the Indian Bean Tree; *Cornus capitata*, a very desirable and tender tree with sensational sulphur-yellow bracts some 4cm. across, followed by strawberry-like fruits in October; magnolias, *M. wilsonii* and *M. acuminata* – the Cucumber Tree. Behind the grotto is a planting of hoherias and the most attractive of all olearias, *O. semidentata* – whose green-grey leaves with silver undersides provide the perfect background to its lilac aster-like flowers with a darker centre, which come out in June.

Through a door set in the south wall is a little bosquet, a secret garden surrounded by box and yew. Between two fine cryptomeria and through a small white gate lies the path to Happy Valley.

A hundred years ago this was the highspot of the Culzean garden. Immaculately kept, a place of tended walks and perpetual interest, now it has reverted to a semi-wild state – and none the worse for that – with an atmosphere of peace and seclusion all its own. This is a spot of great attraction, with many interesting and not a few unusual, trees and shrubs. In perfect shelter, one of the most protected parts of the policies, here are a number of black, secret ponds. Home of *Gunnera manicata* and the Skunk Lily, *Lysichitum (Lysichiton) americanum*, with great yellow spathes, of wild foxgloves and campion and bergenia – and many birds. Huge trees of eucalyptus, the Nootka Cypress (*Chamaecyparis nootkatensis*), first discovered by the Scottish tree-collector Archibald Menzies in

North-West America in 1793; a Sitka Spruce (*Picea sitchensis*) over 20m. high; Wellingtonias; the Giant Fir (*Abies grandis*) and many others.

Near the walled-garden is a group of hybrid tree rhododendrons, *R.* × *altaclarense* (*arboreum*), and elsewhere are fine specimens of *Griselinia littoralis*, tree myrtle, *Olearia macrodonta*, crinodendrons and embothriums, the Chilean Fire Bush, with brilliant scarlet flowers. Cabbage Palms and bamboos give a lush and semi-tropical effect to this delightful valley.

From Happy Valley, a path leads through the woods to the Swan House and its Gothic Aviary, which, after extensive restoration in 1963, now holds birds again. Nearby is the curious octagonal Swan Cottage overlooking the Swan Pond, home of ducks and moorhens and the yellow water-lily (*Nuphar luteum*) The pagoda at the southern end affords a fine view down the length of the water, and in days long past it was possible even to see the Castle from this spot. And so by way of the Cliff Walk back to Culzean Castle.

It could be Culzean's proud boast that there is something for everyone to enjoy: the Adam Castle, so unlike the popular image of his style, containing beautiful rooms and fine pictures and furniture; the 'exotics' on the terraces below the Castle and elsewhere in the woods, groves and gardens; magnificent trees; and the vestiges of a more spacious, leisured age and the results of the estate management of one of the great aristocratic family of 'Improvers' in Scotland.

In 1945 together with the policies and 531 hectares, Culzean became a property of the National Trust for Scotland, through the generosity of the 5th Marquess of Ailsa, and the Adam castle was one of the first great houses to be opened by the Trust. In 1969 the policies and Gardens became a Country Park, managed by the Trust on behalf of the local authorities.

Culzean. The Orangery

5 *top* Culzean. *Olearia semidentata* — a particularly beautiful
shrub and a ready grower on the west coast of Scotland

6 *above* Inverewe. Snow on a tree fern

7 Dawyck. The Dutch Bridge in the Scrape Burn

8 Inverewe. Looking over Loch Ewe to the Torridon Hills

How to get there

On coast 20 km south of AYR; 16 km north of GIRVAN; 6 km west of
MAYBOLE.
A77 north from GIRVAN, turn off left on *A719* at TURNBERRY
A719 south from AYR

FOUR

Dawyck, *Tweedale*

THE WORK of the great 'Improving' lairds across Scotland was by no means confined to agriculture and their gardens; forestry too became a fashionable pastime.

Over the centuries the once fine forests and woodlands in much of Scotland – Pliny's *Silva Caledoniae Vastissima* – had been denuded and carved away. Ship-building, timber for fuel and tannin making had taken a heavy toll. Since the fifteenth century, and perhaps earlier, there had been dire penalties for those who wantonly cut down trees, but these laws had proved ineffective. As indeed had incentives and other persuasions imposed on the tenantry to plant trees on their holdings. By the eighteenth century, in many parts of Scotland, the landscape was bare of trees, in some places even the scrub had been consumed in a continuing orgy of reckless improvidence.

The indigenous trees to Scotland – the oak, birch, alder and Scots pine (*Pinus sylvestris*) – had already been supplemented with others from abroad. In the sixteenth century the Common Spruce (*Picea abies*) had been brought in from Northern Europe, although there are few records of planting in Scotland before the 1680s and 1690s. The European Silver Fir, *Abies alba,* is mentioned by John Evelyn as being introduced to England in 1603, and the first were planted around the 1650s in Scotland. (It is interesting to note that Evelyn had the quaint notion that the Spruce was the male of the species, the Fir the female!) In 1680, the first Cedars of Lebanon (*Cedrus libani*) were introduced. Curiously, in far off times, the tsuga must too have been a native of Scotland as a fossilised cone has been found.

The first commercial crop of trees in Scotland, as opposed to ornamental, screen or landscape planting, is generally considered to be that of European Larch *(Larix decidua)* grown by the great 'Planting Duke' of Atholl at his seat at Blair Atholl in Perthshire. Between 1744 and 1747, no less than 4,000 acres of commercial woodland were planted on the Atholl estates – mainly larch and Scots pine. Other estates were quick to follow this example and across Scotland thousand upon thousand seedling trees were planted in a remarkable burst of afforestation. Some resorted to a more mixed planting incorporating oak and beech (this was particularly so on the lower ground), sometimes elder or elm were added as well.

One of the great pioneer tree enthusiasts in Scotland was Sir James Naesmyth, botanist friend and pupil of the great Linnaeus. His home was at Dawyck in Tweedale and here, in a sheltered glen, in a setting of immense charm, a number of fine specimens of some of these very early trees survive – as well as a fine collection of rhododendrons and other interesting plants of a more recent age. For Dawyck is remarkable, if indeed not unique, in having enjoyed the ownership of three successive, and unrelated families, each of whom in their time was near the forefront of horticultural affairs in Scotland. And, of the greatest interest to tree and rhododendron-lover, the owners of Dawyck subscribed to a great many of the plant-collecting expeditions across the world between the early 1800s to the 1930s – perhaps the most formative years in the history of our garden plants.

Situated in Tweedale near the headwaters of the River Tweed, not far from the little village and Castle of Stobo, Dawyck House stands 200mm. above sea-level in a fold of a hill, the Scrape Hill, whose summit towers to a mighty 695m. behind the house. Down the glen and past Dawyck House, runs the Scrape Burn, which gives the gardens so much of their charm and character, and creates a demi-paradise in spring, summer and autumn.

The soil is nearly lime-free – a good light loam, with excellent drainage. In the glen, years of accumulated leaf-mould, and erosion from above, have created lush conditions in which the Dawyck rhododendrons thrive, but elsewhere the soil is shallow, the rock never far beneath the surface. Rainfall is around 100cm. (40 in.) – half that at another rhododendron garden at Brodick on the Isle of Arran – and drought can be a problem, but frosts and wind are the bane of Dawyck. At this height there is no month of the year when frost has not been recorded, and in a hard winter the thermometer has been known to fall to –14°C (0°F) – although the temperature of –21°C (–4°F) in January, 1941, is still the record. The wind can be as unrelenting – howling down and around the side of Scrape Hill it can do untold damage. The great gale of 1968 blew down over 50,000 trees in the commercial timber plantations and a number of notable trees as well. That in 1973, which struck from the south, a most unusual direction at Dawyck, accounted for several more, amongst them an *Abies nordmanniana*, the Caucasian Fir, of majestic proportions. But the majority survived, and provide the framework for the garden at Dawyck. More than the framework in fact, as without the protection of the great trees it is extremely doubtful if anything would grow on the exposed slopes of the Scrape Glen. It is worth noting that these mighty trees are close-pruned to around 10m., and this canopy provides ideal frost protection for the plants and shrubs beneath.

The earliest-known owners of the Dawyck estate was the family of Veitch (spelt Veache, Vatch, Vaitch, Wach, Wauch or Waugh, according to taste) well known in the Lowlands of Scotland, and with a distinguished public record, but apparently unrelated to the famous nurserymen of that name. In 1691 the estate passed to the no-less eminent family of Naesmyth until, in 1897, it was bought by the grandmother of the present owner, Lieutenant-Colonel A. N. Balfour of Dawyck.

There had been a dwelling on the present site since around 1400, but the former building was almost totally destroyed by fire in 1797. The present house, which was completely rebuilt, dates from 1830. The architect was the eminent Scotsman, William Burn, and it was added to later in the same century by another Scottish architect, John Archibald Campbell. The west wing is an addition dating from 1909 by Sir Robert Lorimer, of Kellie Castle (which will itself feature in a later chapter). The terraces, which are such a feature, were constructed at the same time as the rebuilding of the main house. The observant will notice that each stone pot and finial – and there are over three dozen of them – is fractionally different; the sundial is also of the same workmanship. Little is known of the craftsmen who did the carving except that they were a band of itinerant Italian stonemasons who afterwards carried out similar work at Sir Winston Churchill's house at Chartwell in Kent.

Dawyck's claim to fame in earlier days was its heronry: Dawyck herons provided quarry for the falcons of James IV in the fifteenth century. And in an old account dated 1715 the successors of these birds provided a remarkable phenomenon: 'Here in an old orchard', a traveller wrote, 'did the Herons in my time build their Nests, upon some large Pear-trees. Whereupon in the Harvest time are to be seen much fruit growing and trouts and eels crawling down the body of these trees. These fish the Herons take out of the River Tweed to their Nests and this is the remarkable Riddle that they so much talk of; to have Flesh, Fish and Fruit, at the same time upon one Tree.' For centuries thereafter herons nested at Dawyck, but the gales in the 1968 blew down their nesting trees and they have moved elsewhere.

The same author refers to Naesmyth having 'rebuilt the house and garden and some more ornamental planting for the beauty of the place'. But it was the Veitches who were responsible for the earliest tree planting, and a number of European Silver Firs (*Abies alba*) date from the end of the seventeenth century and one nearly three hundred years old is situated along the glen. However, it is to the Naesmyths that the greater part of the tree planting at Dawyck can be credited. They it was who planted the fine Dutch elms (*Ulmus* x *hollandica* 'Major') which line the present front drive, and the magnificent lime avenue which stretches eastwards for three kilometres. Also in the park to the north-east of the house is a European Larch (*Larix decidua*) planted in 1725 and it is believed that some of the earliest plantings of this tree took place at Dawyck.

The two men who were to have the most far-reaching effect on Scottish, and British forestry, were the Scotsmen Archibald Menzies and David Douglas whose finds in the North-West United States revolutionised ornamental, and commercial conifer planting.

Menzies' trip in 1792, as surgeon-botanist to Captain George Vancouver was responsible for the discovery of many plants and trees. *Zauschneria californica*, the California fuchsia, was one of his finds, *Lupinus arboreus*, the Tree Lupin, another. But it is as the discoverer of two trees in particular that Menzies is best known: *Picea sitchensis*, the Sitka Spruce, the most widely planted conifer in this country today; and *Araucaria araucana*, the Monkey Puzzle, four young plants of which Menzies handed over to his patron Sir Joseph Banks, he having pocketed the nuts at a banquet given in his

Dawyk: The Dutch Bridge.

captain's honour at Valpariso in Chile.

More seeds of this remarkable plant came to this country by the hand of another plant collector, William Lobb, and with the Victorian passion for the exotic and the unusual, it took Britain by storm. From the few plants on the market in the late 1840s each costing upwards of £5, by the 1860s we find that the Monkey Puzzle 'is to be planted in almost every villa . . . the symmetrical outline, the distinct and unusual appearance of the tree . . . causes it to harmonise well with architectural erections, and to be frequently planted in their vicinity; as a single plant on a lawn it has few equals.'

Although Menzies had first discovered the sitka, it was Douglas who introduced this tree, and many others, in any quantity. Sent out by the Royal Horticultural Society, Douglas made a number of extensive exploratory trips between 1823 and 1834 in the North-West corner of America, when during a visit to the Sandwich Islands (Hawaii) he fell into a wild bull pit and was gored to death.

A full list of plants, shrubs and trees introduced by Douglas is vast; his influence on our gardens, even today, enormous. Among his better known importations as *Ribes sanguinea*, the widely planted 'Flowering Currant', which achieved huge popularity in Britain;

Garrya elliptica, one of the most magnificent of all evergreens, with shiny leathery leaves and great greyish-green catkins; *Mahonia aquifolium, Mimulus moschatus,* the little musk plant which soon ousted the mignonette as the most popular scented plant in drawing-room and cottage alike, until, around the turn of the nineteenth century, it was noticed that the musk had lost its smell, not only in the cultivated plants, but in the wild as well. This is one of the great unsolved plant mysteries.

But it is as a tree collector that Douglas is best known. 'You will begin to think', Douglas wrote to his great friend Sir William Hooker, Director of Kew, 'that I manufacture Pines at my pleasure.' And a glance at the list of Douglas' conifer introductions explains what he means. *Abies procera (nobilis),* the Noble Fir; *Abies amabilis,* the Red Silver Fir; *Abies grandis,* the Giant Fir; *Pinus ponderosa,* the Western Yellow Pine; *Pinus contorta,* the Beach Pine; *Pinus coulteri,* the Big Cone Pine, discovered by a Dr Coulter 1832 and introduced by Douglas the same year; *Pinus lambertiana,* the Sugar Pine; *Pinus radiata,* the Monterey Pine; in fact Douglas discovered seven of the seventeen pines that are known to exist on the Pacific Coast. It is also believed that he first identified the Monterey Cypress, (*Cupressus macrocarpa*) although any seed he sent back, if indeed he did, became lost and the introduction of this widely grown tree is normally attributed to another tree-collector Karl Theodore Hartweg. But it is as the introducer of the great 'Douglas' Fir that David Douglas is best known. First seen by Menzies who collected pressed specimens as he sailed up the Pacific coast of America, stopping here and there on the way, the Douglas Fir was introduced to cultivation by Douglas in 1825.

Naesmyth of Dawyck was a contributor to a number of the expeditions to Western America and the Far East around this time, and many of the finest trees at Dawyck owe their origin to seed collected by Douglas and the other plant hunters. Prominent among them is of course the Oregon Douglas Fir, *Pseudotsuga menziesii* planted in 1838; the tallest Douglas in the Glen is 48m. at most recent measurement. One specimen of *Pinus jeffreyi* also dates from 1838, which is very considerably earlier than the usual introduction date attributed to this species, and an example of *Tsuga heterophylla,* the Western Hemlock, was planted in 1860. This tree was discovered as early as 1826 by Douglas but not introduced until 1851 when Jeffrey, yet another Scottish tree-collector, sent back seed to Scotland.

DAWYCK

Lime
Avenue

1. Dawyck House
2. Dawyck Beech
3. Old Larch
4. Walled Garden
5. Beech Walk
6. Rhododendron Walk
7. Chapel Walk

8. Chapel
9. Scrape Burn
10. Dutch Bridge
11. Sycamore Walk
12. Old Gateway

Of almost as great interest as Naesmyth's successes were his failures, all of which were faithfully recorded. In this he makes claim to have been the first to plant *Pinus nigra,* the Austrian Pine, which was introduced by the great tree nursery of Messrs Lawson of Edinburgh, and *Pinus ponderosa,* the Douglas introduction. His failures, many of which have been echoed since, include *Pinus pinea,* the Umbrella or Stone Pine – his notes say 'many tried, but they won't grow here', hardly surprising as it is a native of the Mediterranean coast; equally predictable were his failures with *Pinus halepensis,* the Aleppo Pine; but his failures with some others are interesting, eg. *Pinus lambertiana,* the Sugar Pine, and *Pinus sabiniana,* the Digger Pine, both introduced by Douglas, and *Picea morinda,* the West Himalayan Spruce. Of the latter Naesmyth dolefully records: 'All have died here.' He failed too with *Cedrus deodara,* the Deodar, whereas the present owner has now succeeded.

Dawyck is probably best known in tree circles for the Dawyck Beech, the fastigiate form of the common beech (*Fagus sylvatica*) The story behind this remarkable tree is that one day Naesmyth was walking in a plantation of young beech and noticed a peculiarly fastigiate form growing among the ordinary variety. The rogue was removed to a position south of the house and allowed to grow in peace – and grow it did, maintaining its fastigiate form throughout. The original tree is now 24m. high, but it sets no seed and must be vegetatively propagated. So that every Dawyck beech across the world can be said to have derived from this one specimen. The Dawyck Beech, more properly *Fagus sylvatica* 'Dawyck' ('Fastigiata'), attained the ultimate in horticultural recognition when in 1969 in was given an Award of Garden Merit by the Royal Horticultural Society.

It is to F. R. S. Balfour, father of the present owner, that the form and much of the content of the garden is owed. Business took Fred Balfour, as he was always affectionately known, to North West America and here he acquired an everlasting love for the conifers he had first known in his home in Scotland. He started to collect in earnest, bringing back plants and seed, which he would get down from the uppermost branches with a catapult, with which he was something of an expert. One tree which Balfour was particularly anxious to get hold of was *Picea brewerana,* Brewer's Weeping Spruce, a tree of immense beauty with long branches. This tree was discovered in 1891 growing in a few isolated localities in the Siskyou Mountains of South Oregon, and when Balfour became interested it was extremely rare in cultivation. He therefore set out to find it, and after three days' gruelling trek, came across two small groves several kilometres apart. He prevailed upon a local settler, to whom he had done a service, to send him some plants, and in due course fourteen specimens arrived alive at Dawyck. One of which can be seen west of the house on the path towards the church. It was planted in 1908.

In later years, he started to subscribe to the many plant-collecting expeditions then being sent out under Wilson, Forrest, Kingdon-Ward and others. Gradually a remarkably comprehensive collection of trees and shrubs began to accumulate – some to thrive, some to perish – but a considerable number of these early introductions still survive at Dawyck.

It was shortly before the First World War that Balfour became interested in rhododendrons; he was one of the founder members of the Rhododendron Society in 1915. He had already brought in a number of Western American rhododendrons from his travels, including *R. vaseyi,* the original plant of which is in the glen; and the Naesmyths had been responsible for a few – *R. ponticum* and ponticum hybrids chiefly, but also some very old *R. maximum* and *R. catawbiense,* the former of which is still alive. Now, with the help and generosity of Professors Bailey Balfour at Edinburgh and Charles Sprague Sargent at the Arnold Arboretum in the United States, the Dawyck collection increased in size and interest, including the products of E. H. (Chinese) Wilson's rhododendron expeditions in 1907 and 1908. Losses have been heavy in the unkind climate of Dawyck, and a number of earlier introductions vanished during the war years, but there are now over 120 different species of rhododendron at Dawyck, as well as innumerable hybrids.

First to flower, in late February or early March, is *R. fulgens,* but more often than not the bright scarlet bell-shaped flowers are destroyed by frost. Next follow *RR. sutchuense, calophytum, fargesii* and *oreodoxa,* all in March: these members of the fortunei series normally escape the worst of the frosts, but are inclined to slight damage. April sees the appearance of the rare *R. russotinctum,* a taliense. Other members of this series – all particularly hardy and in flower at the same time, include *RR. adenogynum, balfourianum* and *bureavii,* an outstanding rhododendron particularly for its beautiful young growth and dark, glossy green leaves with their thick rich red woolly indumentum; there are many plants of *R. bureavii* dotted about the garden. Others include *R. clementinae* and *R. wasonii* – a particularly desirable rhododendon in its rarer yellow form, the neat, glossy foliage above is a beautiful contrast with the clear white indumentum below, which turns a bright rusty red with age. Another species flowering at this time at Dawyck is *R. lacteum,* of which there are two plants growing near the Dutch Bridge at the top of the glen. This is normally considered of weak constitution, but here the plants survive well although the delicate yellow flowers are often nipped by frost. This form is a very good clear yellow without blotches. The lacteum series is also represented by *R. wightii,* with cream-coloured, one-sided trusses, this is much hardier than is general in this series.

R. campanulatum also flowers here in April. The Dawyck plants are a good clear blue, and the form known as *aeruginosum* is well worth growing for the magnificent metallic-blue-green sheen on the leaves which deepens with age finally turning a soft blue. Among the neriiflorum series, note should be taken of *R. citriniflorum,* a fairly rare species in cultivation which belongs to the sub-series sanguineum. This rhododendron has striking lemon-yellow flowers shaded a deep orange at the base. There are two bushes near the Scrape Burn.

May is the month when a late frost can normally be expected at Dawyck, but provided the temperature remains above –4°C (25°F) most of the flowers survive undamaged. This is the time when the Dawyck rhododendrons are at their best. Most of the triflorums are now in full bloom, including *RR. ambiguum, davidsonianum, amesii, augustinii* – a truly magnificent plant this, one of the finest of the blues – and others. Towards the end of the month is the turn of the best of the thomsonii series, particularly a very fine plant of *R. williamsianum.* Fully 3m. across and 1.5m. high, this is a consistent flowerer and the delightful shell-pink flowers against the small, heart-shaped leaves provides one of the sights of Dawyck. This plant is on the left of the main patch up the glen. Another pride of Dawyck are the specimens of *R. souliei*; these used to be scattered around the garden but they have now been brought together in a group on the right halfway up the main glen path. The six or seven plants with flowers varying from the purest white to a deep pink create a magnificent display. This is one of the rhododendrons which certainly seems to do better in Scotland away from the west coast. Another rhododendron of particular merit and which always seems to escape the frost is *R. argyrophyllum* of the arboreums – a good plant this with clear pink flowers and silver-felted leaves beneath.

June sees *R. insigne,* another with beautiful metallic-coloured leaves. This too escapes, or is never damaged by frost. Among others now in flower are *R. cinnabarinum,* and its variety *R.c. roylei,* the gem of the lot with flowers of a wonderful deep purplish bright red, and glaucous leaves. While among the azaleas, *R. arborescens* with white flowers shading to pink and a wonderful scent is particularly noteworthy. Latest to flower is *R. ungernii,* a member of the ponticum series with funnel-shaped pink-white flowers and leathery leaves with greyish-white tomentose beneath.

A feature of Dawyck in spring are the daffodils. Each year for twenty years the father of the present owner planted one ton of bulbs, so they have been naturalised for decades and a continuous regeneration goes on with new varieties introduced each year. The result is breathtaking and the sight of these sheets of yellow and white against the black of a flock of Welsh Mountain sheep is a picture to remember.

South of the house lie the terraces and immediately behind is a broad avenue rising toward the summit of Scrape Hill. To the west, the Scrape Burn twists and tumbles its way past the house. An attractive stone bridge links the house with the gardens and one of the attractions of Dawyck is how the formality of house, lawn and terrace merges into the informality of the glen.

Along the marshy edge of the stream are azaleas and a number of other interesting plants. A purple-leaved rhubarb, *Rheum palmatum* sends up its metre-long panicles of red flowers in June. *Lysichitum (Lysichiton) americanum* – the Skunk Lily – makes its decaying presence known very pungently, and its less well-known brother *L. camtschatcense,* with attractive white spathes and a considerably better smell, grows nearby. Primulas do not do well at Dawyck, but their absence is more than made up for by a fine range of trillium – *T. grandiflorum* and *T. erectum* and others, and which are happiest in what full sun there is. The Meconopsis is another successful plant at Dawyck, particularly the deepest blue *M. × sheldonii.*

Walking up the glen beneath the impressive canopy of the great trees of Dawyck is a delightful experience. The path is flanked with rhododendrons, *Pieris japonica* and *P. floribunda* (*P. formosa forrestii* will not, however, grow at Dawyck), and other shrubs and small trees:

acers, sorbus and prunus are among the best represented species, but others abound. An unusual ilex, *I. fargesii,* from West China, normally considered only a large shrub is here a tree some 8m. tall. Its narrow leaves and small red fruits are distinctive and attractive, and the tree stands near the charming Dutch Bridge, built by a Dutchman in 1830, which spans the burn at the top of the glen. On the other side of the water near a good *Cercidiphyllum japonicum* is an excellent and little-known acer, *A. heldreichii,* with deeply-cleft leaves like a Virginian Creeper and a sensational autumn colour. Along this same path and opposite the Brewer's Weeping Spruce mentioned before, stands a large alder, *Alnus sinuata,* with immensely-long catkins in spring before the leaves appear. Below, on the glenside near a specimen of the fastigiate cypress oak, *Quercus robur* 'Fastigiata', stands a tree with the beautiful mahogany bark of *Prunus serrula;* this is *Betula forrestii.* Another, with similar bark, is *Prunus dawyckensis,* brought back as seed from the Wilson expedition of 1907, it was first flowered at Dawyck, and is possibly a hybrid *(P. canescens × P. dielsiana).*

Passing back again over the Dutch Bridge past a group of *Rhododendron* 'Circe' and a fine *Prunus × yedoensis,* a path leads upwards to the Beech Walk. This is a completely sheltered spot, a place to linger, from where the best view of the house and the glen may be obtained. At the end are a number of noteworthy trees; a sensational bluish-grey *Abies magnifica,* the Californian Red Fir; and an equally-fine specimen of *Abies delavayi georgei* from West China, introduced as recently as 1923; as well as a splendid Noble Fir, *Abies procera,* the oldest *procera* were planted at Dawyck in 1850.

Below the original Dawyck beech, are two of the fine collection of sorbus in the garden, *S. discolor,* with cream-coloured fruits, and *S. scalaris* with small red fruits in a tight compact flat head, a distinctive wide-spreading habit and fern-like foliage; as well as an unusual maple, *Acer giraldii,* and the rare *A. nipponicum* which grows near the burn.

But no visit to Dawyck can be complete without a walk down the great Lime Avenue to look back at the house and the noble trees of the glen. While here a trip should be made to the neat walled-garden with its attractive Italian wellhead, whose origin is unknown, climbing roses, herbaceous borders and greenhouses – for Dawyck is a garden of many aspects. A garden to remember.

How to get there

13 km south-west of PEEBLES; 16 km east of BIGGAR
B7016 east from BIGGAR – right on to *A701* – after 3 km left on to
B712

or

A72 west from PEEBLES – or turn left after 6 km turn left on to *B712*

FIVE

Inverewe   *Ross-shire*

THE RHODODENDRON gardens of the West Coast are to many the typical Scottish garden. Made possible by the warming airs of the North Atlantic Drift and a heavy rainfall (at Inverewe, the most famous of all Scottish gardens, this can be more than 150cm. (60in.) a year) on the west coast of Britain, in Cornwall and from the Solway Firth northwards, are the conditions beloved by rhododendrons, and they thrive. None of these gardens in Scotland are much over 100 years old, and many are a good deal younger, yet their creation marked as great a revolution in garden style as the transition from the formal to the landscape form in the latter part of the previous century in England.

By the 1850s, the strict formality in gardens of the Victorian era was in full sway. The meticulous intricacies of the formal bedding scheme, when armies of gardeners raised half-hardy annual plants by the tens of thousand, was at his height. The stereotype gardens of the great houses vied with each other to produce grander and more eye-catching schemes: formality without beauty, extravagance without value, one critic called it. Plants were regimented with little regard to their natural habit, which was inhibited in the interest of geometrical nicety. The smaller gardens, owned by the burgeoning middle classes, aped their larger brethren to produce beds and borders of garish colours and petit-point detail – forgetting that the formal bedding scheme required, above all, space if it were not to overwhelm by sheer magnificence.

Yet this was the beginning of the great age of plant introductions, and Kew, under the incomparable Sir William Hooker, was getting into its stride. The interchange of plants and plant material across

the world reached colossal proportions and the importance of
economic botany assumed new dimensions as Kew sponsored the
introduction of plants which revolutionised the economies of the host
nations – rubber to Malaya; Chinchona, the quinine plant, to India;
tea to Assam, and many others.

Species by the hundred were now reaching these shores through
the medium of such plant-hunters as William Lobb and Richard
Pearce who, in South America, braved the hazard of 'a jaguar every
yard', not to say terrible disease; Ernest Dieffenbach in New
Zealand; John Reeves in China, and many others. Some of their
plants were sent to musty, impersonal herbaria, some to the botanic
gardens which were enjoying the surge of popular enthusiasm for
anything scientific, some to those who sponsored the expeditions.

For the most part, the new arrivals were stove plants – to satisfy
the insatiable Victorian appetite for greenhouse culture – or
half-hardy plants suitable for bedding schemes, or, most desirable of
all, the 'curiosities' those bizarre and peculiar plants in which the
Victorians took particular, often morbid, delight. Such as the
carnivorous Pitcher Plants or the Sumatran Giant Arum, a monster
as big as a small car which, whenever it flowered – a mercifully rare
event – stank reeking 'of the effluvia of all drains and all corruption'
(as one newspaper choicely described its glory). But there were
many of what we would call hardy perennials and shrubs as well,
and as more and more horticulturists saw the garden potential of
the new plants, a revolt against the formal garden began to gather
momentum.

The new plants could not in many cases fall into the scheme of
formal bedding, nor fit into the Victorian shrubbery of ornamental
evergreen, of laurel, yew, the Portuguese laurel and *Rhododendron
ponticum*. Some gardeners, particularly those near the west coast,
experimented with the hardiness of the new arrivals, and were often
agreeably surprised, but in the main they were classed as 'too
difficult' and left to the botanic gardens. Exception was made of
some American and South African importations, and by the early
1800s the azalea, kalmia and some ericas were well established on
the British gardening scene. The ancestor of the 'Wild Garden' was
beginning to take shape.

But generally, by the middle of the nineteenth century, the heavy
stultifying hand of the Victorian formal gardener had fallen
throughout these islands; and a geometrical lack of imagination

9 Inverewe. *Cordyline indivisa* — a tender 'cabbage tree' from New Zealand

10 Crathes Castle. A view from the upper floor showing the massive yew hedge and, below, the Rose Garden, in the centre of which is a particularly fine specimen of *Stranvaesia davidiana*

closed remorselessly on the garden scene. An exception lay in the Victorian enthusiasm for conifers which were avidly collected; the first pinetum in Scotland was created in 1830.

The event which was to break the stranglehold of the Victorian bedding scheme in Scotland, was the introduction in the early 1850s of the large-leaved rhododendrons. Credit for this milestone in gardening belongs almost exclusively to one man, Joseph Hooker, son of Sir William, who in 1847 was commissioned by Kew to collect plants in India. As his instructions were to compare the Antarctic flora, with which he was already familiar from his experiences when Captain Ross' expedition to the southern continent seven years before, with that of the High Himalayas, he was advised to make for Sikkim in the north-east corner of India. It was a fortunate choice, for it was in Sikkim that Hooker found the first of the large-leaved rhododendrons which were to form the basis of the collections in many rhododendron gardens in this country, and of the many hybrids which have made the rhododendron so popular today. It is not too much to say that Sir Joseph Hooker – he succeeded his father as Director of Kew in 1865 and was knighted 12 years later for his services to botany – is the father of the modern rhododendron. It is sometimes forgotten that *Rhododendron griffithianum (aucklandii)*, and *RR. dalhousiae, falconeri, hodgsonii* and *thomsonii*, species of immense importance in the evolution of the modern rhododendron, were all early Hooker importations.

The Hookers had long owned a country cottage at the head of Holy Loch and he was familiar with the climate on the west coast of Scotland. So, believing that if any climate was to prove amenable to the new Sikkim rhododendrons it must be here, and in Cornwall, seeds and plants were given to their many friends in the area. Even he would have been surprised at the success of the experiment.

For the success was outstanding: the Sikkim rhododendrons grew almost as well as those in their native country. They were magnificent plants and the exciting potential of the large-leaved rhododendrons and other peat-loving plants attracted one of the great personalities in Scottish gardening – Osgood Mackenzie.

The Mackenzies had lived for many generations in Wester Ross, that remote, at times almost inaccessible, piece of Scotland on the north-west coast. Bred and brought up in that inhospitable part of the highlands, the Mackenzies were as tough and as independent as

Myosotidium hortensia (nobile), *the Chatham Islands Forget-me-not.*

any Highlander. And toughness was needed as much as imagination in the creation of Inverewe. It is difficult for the visitor to believe as he walks around the soft glades and braes of Inverewe that this gardening haven actually lies at the same latitude as Labrador and is slightly further north than Moscow.

In 1862 Osgood Mackenzie was given a piece of land by his mother. It was a barren peninsula no more than a few hectares in extent, known as Am Ploc Ard (the Gaelic for the High Lump). The only growth was the ubiquitous heather and one stunted willow, which survived for many years – a plant of curiosity and legend – but has now disappeared. There was no protection from the wind, which always blew, and only the low, whale-back of the Island of Lewis lay between Inverewe and the full fury of the Atlantic Ocean. As uncompromising as the wind was the soil, a thin layer varying from 5cm. to 60cm. of black soggy peat overlying red Torridonian sandstone – outcrops of this rock can be seen in many parts of the garden. The sole redeeming feature was that this rock was in many places rotten and crumbled easily. It was on this daunting prospect that Osgood Mackenzie decided to build his garden.

The first requirement was to construct a fence across the neck of the peninsula – then to build a windbreak, and in 1864 a thick belt of Corsican pine and Scots fir was planted. Many of these same trees survive today. Bowed and weather-beaten, no more than 12-13m.

high, stained with salt and with many of the lower branches bleached and petrified, they served and still serve their purpose. Within the shelter they provide lies a paradise which each year attracts close on 130,000 visitors.

The achievement is awe-inspiring, Osgood Mackenzie's vision remarkable, his persistence astonishing. For not until 15 years had passed could any real planting take place. Then were introduced the eucalyptus, the rhododendrons and many other plants which make Inverewe a place of pilgrimage for so many gardeners.

The gardens today, although owing their origin to Osgood Mackenzie, were also the creation of Mairi Sawyer, Mackenzie's daughter, and of Dr J. M. Cowan who after a long career as Assistant Regius Keeper of the Royal Botanic Garden in Edinburgh retired to Inverewe in 1954, to spend the remainder of his days in a garden he had already come to know and to love.

Mairi Sawyer took on the task when her father died in 1922, and the present framework of the garden owes much to her. She was, in her way as much a legend in Wester Ross as had been her parent. She was a formidable and much loved personality, a worthy successor and soon as knowledgeable as her notable father, and in 1952 it was she, with great generosity, who gifted the great garden to the National Trust for Scotland.

The first taste of the unusual and exotic at Inverewe greets the visitor at the Gate Lodge. Here, growing luxuriantly, is the Chilean *Crinodendron hookerianum,* which has the curious habit of pushing out its flower-stalks in the autumn, although the flowers do not open until the following summer – and, *Olearia semidentata,* both of a delicate constitution in less favourable climes. Stretching away towards the modern house runs The Drive, bounded on the seaward side with a clipped hedge of *Rhododendron ponticum* above the walled-garden, on the other by a long border, the home of many exciting plants and shaded by magnificent specimens of *Eucalyptus coccifera,* and other trees. Here is a planting of heather and St Daboec's Heath, *Daboecia cantabrica,* a native of the West of Ireland. Particular note should be made of a colossal camellia which is said to be nearly 200 years old and which was bought by Osgood Mackenzie in a house sale a hundred years ago for one shilling. A number of South African plants dwell happily here, and with no protection, *Agapanthus oreintalis (umbellatus),* and its white variant,

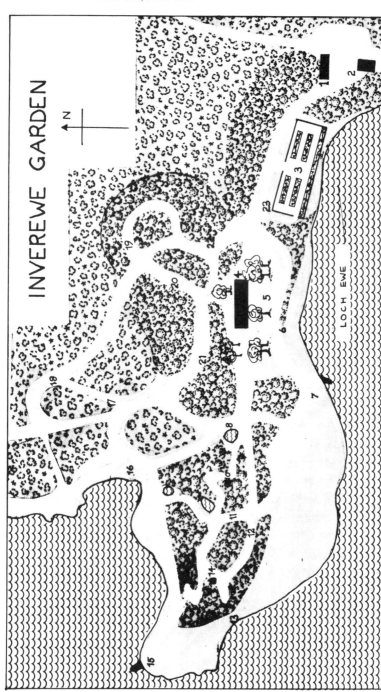

INVEREWE GARDEN

N

LOCH EWE

1. Lodge
2. Information Centre
3. Walled Garden
4. Inverewe House
7. Japan
8. Small Pond and
   Peat Banks
9. Crocs a hias
13. View Point
14. Second Shelter Hut
15. Cuddy Rock and Jetty
    and Peace Plot
19. Bambooselem
20. Rhododendron Walk

and 'Headbourne Hybrids', which are generally hardier than the species; as well as Watsonias, a member of the iris family resembling a gladiolus. Behind, is a fine *Eucryphia* x *nymansensis* 'Nymansay', whose huge white flowers wreath the branches in late summer, and *E. glutinosa*, which flowers somewhat earlier and whose leaves colour beautifully in the autumn. Sensational too, are the hoherias, *H. lyalli* and *H. glabrata* with their cherry-like pendant white blossoms in early summer. A number of rhododendrons flourish here too, among them *RR. oreotrephes, falconeri* and the superb *thomsonii*, with deep-red flowers and plum-coloured bark – the last two being Hooker introductions. Behind this border is *R. ciliatum*, a member of the generally delicate Maddenii series, whose rose-coloured flowers come out in March and which can be relied upon to flower well as a young plant. This rhododendron is planted all along the path behind the border, and is well worth a short detour at the right season.

The path now passes the Myosotidium bed, where a broad sheet of the vivid blue *Myosotidium hortensia (nobile)* Forget-me-not (Chatham Island, East of New Zealand) may be seen in April and May. This is the plant most associated with Inverewe and for years it mouldered, until, as Mairi Sawyer described in an article in the RHS Journal 'I saw a letter in *The Times* from a sailor who had seen this giant forget-me-not on the shores of the Chatham Islands growing in rotten seaweed and sharks' carcasses. It took little time for me to collect seaweed on the adjacent shore and herring-fry from the ebb-tide and soon after the plants were surrounded with these, they began to flourish, and have never looked back.'

To the right of the present house, which was rebuilt in 1937, is an area known as America. Here in the well-drained conditions near an enormous *Eucalyptus coccifera* are a number of exciting plants. Including a variegated Turkey Oak, *Quercus cerris* 'Variegata,' a very fast grower, with highly decorative white margins to the leaves. Terrestial orchids flourish, among them the Algerian, *Orchis elata* with 60cm. stems. Gentians, the blue and white varieties of the Willow Gentian *Gentiana asclepiadea,* and the gem of the family *G. sino-ornata*. Two variegated hollies *Ilex aquifolium* 'Golden Queen' and 'Silver Queen', and rhododendrons, the early-flowering hybrid 'Blue Tit' and the species *RR. haematodes, orbiculare, williamsianum* and many others.

Now the visitor's feet will take him away from the sea shore, and the wonderful atmosphere of Inverewe starts to make its true impact. The lush, sometimes almost tropical growth, the pervading scent of damp earth and moss and the fragrance of rhododendron and azalea. The buzz of bees in the blossom and, perhaps, the staccato patter of raindrops on the flat rhododendron leaves. The 'presence' of Inverewe is unique, it is a place to talk in whispers, and one authority has likened it to 'some wild corner in Burma or Northern China'.

The quaintly-titled Bambooselem will next draw the visitor. Here, amid the bamboos which give the place its name, is one of the prides of Inverewe, an enormous *Magnolia campbellii*. Planted in the 1920s, it is now nearly 12m. high. Naturally a tardy flowerer – it does not produce flowers until it is 20-30 years old – this one is an unforgettable sight in spring with its huge deep pink saucers 20cm. across on the leafless branches. This is not the only noteworthy plant in Bambooselem. Here too are rhododendrons, a plant of the Chusan palm, *Trachycarpus fortunei; Buddleia colvilei,* with conspicuous sprays of red flowers; *Embothrium coccineum;* enkianthus and the winter-flowering *Azara integrifolia browneae,* with yellow flowers and obovate leaves. This is a Chilean species and is more normally grown as a wall shrub. And in the moist soil other plants thrive: lilies, *LL. auratum, martagon,* the American *michiganense,* and the architectural Giant Lily, *Cardiocrinum giganteum,* over two metres tall. There is also a little known Madeiran native, *Geranium anemonifolium,* with blue cranesbill flowers on long, robust stalks, 60cm. long over a broad crown of anemone-shaped soft green leaves. A plant hardier than is generally supposed.

Past groups and drifts of meconopsis, primulas and trilliums, the path leads to what is known as Peace Plot, which was originally planted after the First World War. It is, appropriately enough, one of the most sheltered spots in all Inverewe. Here is the home of *Rhododendron* 'Fragrantissimum', one of the choicest of choice rhododendrons, and other equally tender members of the Maddenii series, as well as some of the better hybrids, including, the satin-pink 'Naomi Pink Beauty', and the beautiful sulphur-yellow Exbury hybrid 'Hawk'. On the floor are trollius, the globe flower, and, in profusion, primulas. The sickle-shaped leaves of *Iris kaempferi* vie with meconopsis, and in spring the whole is carpeted with the dog-tooth violet, *Erythronium revolutum* 'White Beauty'. An unusual tree is *Kalopanax pictus (Acanthopanax ricinifolius),* which bears some resemblance to a maple, but as a member of Araliaceae carries formidable thorns; it has clusters of white flowers in the autumn.

And so to the Rhododendron Walk. Here are the large-leaved rhododendrons, *R. sinogrande* and *R. hodgsonii,* among them, the former a huge tree 9m. high, and as many wide. A giant *Drimys winteri* dominates one point, a Scarlet Willow, *Salix alba* 'Chryostella', with brilliant scarlet branches in the winter months, focusses attention on another. In autumn, the herbaceous Umbrella Plant, *Peltiphyllum peltatum* makes its presence known with a sensational display of colour. This, a member of the saxifrage family, with palmate leaves agm. wide white flowers, hails from California and delights in a watery situation.

From here the walker's way will probably take him to one of the highest features on the peninsula, Coronation Knoll, which commemorates the Coronation of Queen Elizabeth the Second. This is where the many seedling rhododendrons found around Inverewe are put out to try their luck and prove their worth. Other planting has also taken place here and in the next door Pender's Walk the observant will find *Acacia melanoxylon*; the pea-flowered *Sophora tetraptera*, and azaras both *A. serrata* and *A. lanceolata.*

The north-west side of Inverewe, near an area called Camas Glas (The Grey Bay), bore the brunt of the devastating gale in 1953 which did so much damage. This has now been extensively cleared and planted with rhododendron and sorbus. There is also a specimen of *Eucalyptus dalrympleana* which does well here – others which will grow include *E.E. gunnii, coccifera, pauciflora* and *cordata*. In spring, beneath poplar and willow, bright patches of purple may be seen, this is from the root parasite *Lathraea clandestina.*

Passing a bare face of the red sandstone up which scrambles the Japanese *Schizophragma hydrangeoides* – a climber which is too little seen in gardens, with round coarsely-toothed leaves and flower heads which can reach eighteen inches across – one emerges on the Cuddy Rock, the very tip of An Ploc Ard. Here one is surrounded by olearias, which can best withstand the rigours of the sea exposure.

From the shade of the Shelter Hut the visitor can look down on the glory of the Large Pond, a sheet of multi-coloured water-lilies, the chestnut-shaped leaf of rodgersias; irises and hostas. And it is but a step to what is known as the High Viewpoint which on a clear day affords a magnificent panorama of the Wester Ross scenery – the shadowy Torridon range of mountains to the south, the little town of

Poolewe in a corner of the Loch and to the west the grey anonymity of the Atlantic Ocean.

The visitor is now on the return journey; but what a journey. First he will pass drifts of azaleas, in May and June the air heavy with scent and the noise of myriad bees going about their business. A number of species of rhododendrons lead him to the appropriately-named Wet Valley. The shiny foliage and yellow spathes of the Skunk Lily *Lysichitum (Lysichiton) americanum* menace one corner, the huge leaves of *Gunnera manicata* monopolise another, while the keen-eyed may notice the dark-green kidney-shaped leaves of its four-inch relative *G. magellanica* growing beside it in ridiculous comparison. Here also can be found the interesting hybrid *Ourisia* 'Loch Ewe'. The ourisias are a useful and decorative family of garden and front-of-the-border plants hailing, some from New Zealand but the majority from the Andes. The pink 'Loch Ewe' was raised by crossing the scarlet South American *O. coccinea* with the white New Zealand *O. macrophylla,* a delightful pink has resulted.

Ahead lies Crag a Lios, a natural rockgarden. Here are more ourisias and large plantings of the candelabra primula, *P. pulverulenta*. Nearby can be seen the scarlet and yellow tubular flowers of *Desfontainia spinosa,* which set against the rich shiny holly-like foliage makes one of nature's finest combinations. Also a number of highly desirable rhododendrons; *R. maddenii,* the rich-red *R. griersonianum* hybrid *R. 'Elizabeth',* somewhat hardier than its parent, and some excellent triflorums.

From Crag a Lios one passes to the Peat Border and Small Pond where sheets of primulas and meconopsis cover the ground in early summer. Here the Far Eastern *Iris laevigata,* and other plants, thrive in and near the water, including a North American pitcher-plant *Sarracenia purpurea* which produces evil greenish-purple flowers in April, and another moisture lover, *Shortia uniflora* from Japan, with pink flowers set against round pale green leaves which colour well in the autumn – the whole a bare 10cm. high. Autumn colour is a feature; the genus *Sorbus* is represented by *SS. hupehensis, sargentiana* and *vilmorinii,* while the lime-hating *Fothergilla major* creates a splash of orange, yellow and red in season. At the rear is an uncommon clematis, *C. × vedrariensis* a cross between *C. chrysocoma* and *C. montana rubens* with the colour of the latter but with broader sepals.

Now comes Japan – an area named after a pink cherry which used to reside here. This is a treasury of delicate shrubs: a mimosa, *Acacia dealbata* seems wholly happy; *Callistemon linearis,* a red Bottle Brush; *Gevuina avellana,* the Chilean Hazel with highly-polished bright green pinnate leaves and white flowers; and two different kinds of Australian Tree Fern, the large *Dicksonia artarctica* with fronds 1.5 metres or even 1.8 metres long, and the smaller *D. squarrosa* with fronds a bare 30 to 35 cm. in length.

North of Japan is an area flattened by the 1953 gales which is replanting itself by natural regeneration. And tucked into a corner grows a *Rhododendron giganteum,* the largest of the species. This plant has been grown from seed sent 50 years ago by the great Scottish plant-hunter George Forrest. A wooden cross-section which shows the size of *R. giganteum* in the wild is in the Information Hut, this too was a present from George Forrest.

And so to the area of Inverewe House where most conspicuous is a grove of large trees west of the building – *Cryptomeria japaonica*; a Wellingtonia, *Sequoiadendron giganteum;* Silver Firs, *Abies alba;* and a fine Lawson's Cypress *Chamaecyparis lawsoniana.* Below the house and the terrace lawn, is the Rock Garden where many delightful and unusual plants can be found. The celmisias are distinctive with their striking silver-grey leaves and daisy flowers; *Daphne arbuscula* and *D. retusa* scent the air; cyclamen are in profusion, gentians, omphalodes, the vivid pink *Oxalis enneaphylla* and many other noteworthy rock plants. Over all, swaying in the soft winds off Loch Ewe, are the Fairy Wands of *Dierama pulcherrima.*

Conveniently placed nearby are some benches. Here is a place to rest awhile and think about this beautiful garden. To ponder and wonder at the genius, the perseverance, above all the vision of the man who created this little paradise on a once-barren peninsula.

How to get there

137 km north-west of INVERNESS; 58 km north-west of
ACHNASHEEN

A9 west from INVERNESS – after 21 km turn left on to *A832*

SIX

Kellie Castle *Fife*

As THE Hooker rhododendrons were to break the spell of Victorian rigidity in Scotland, at least on the west coast, elsewhere, by the 1870s, a new and formidable opponent of the Victorian bedding scheme was making his mark on the garden scene. This was William Robinson. Born in 1839, he had achieved, by the time of his death 97 years later, perhaps the greatest transition in garden design in the history of gardening: the extremes of the Victorian-style formal bedding were long dead and buried.

He was an irascible, often inconsistent Irishman. The story – or perhaps legend – of his appearance in the gardening world has often been told: how, in a fit of pique, he abandoned his employer's hothouses one frosty night, leaving their lights open and their fires damped, and walked to Dublin to seek employment with that colossus of botany, David Moore, at the Glasnevin Botanic Garden. How Moore befriended him, and sent him to London to work at the Royal Botanic Society's garden in Regent's Park. How he then turned to his true metier, as a horticultural journalist.

It was Robinson's third book, *The Wild Garden*, published in 1870, that set the gardening world to wonder and started the avalanche which was to engulf the Victorian formal garden. Touchy and irrational as Robinson undoubtedly was, there is equally no doubt that he was a very far-seeing gardener with a highly pungent and literate force of persuasion.

When working in London, he had been fascinated by the little cottage gardens in the villages in the counties around. So natural, so uninhibited, so completely in contrast with the niggling formality of the Victorian garden. Gradually, Robinson's concept of the natural garden developed: cottage garden in style and atmosphere, but using the wealth of new plants, the perennials, the semi-shrubs, those many plants beautiful in themselves which would not, or could not, be dragooned or tortured to conform with the seried heights and habit demanded of them by the gardeners of the day.

Using his gardening magazines, Robinson poured scorn and invective on the 'Pastry-work garden' and the 'intolerable need of digging up the garden twice a year'. He was no less scathing with the gardener who littered the scene with unnecessary statuary, and with the 'fountain-monger'.

Robinson's campaign reached its peak when, in November, 1883, he published the *English Flower Garden* – possibly the most formative book in the history of garden design – and with its appearance the demise of the Victorian formal garden was certain. Robinson's timing turned out to be exquisite, for rising wages had tolled the end of the huge formal garden, and the new plants which were entering the country in their hundreds, proved particularly suitable for the new-style suburban garden.

Prior to this, in 1875, Robinson had met another pioneer in gardening history, Gertrude Jekyll. It was she who tempered the 'Wild' school of gardening and who married concept and design to the 'feel' of the house. In her hands Unity of Design gained a new interpretation, and her literacy was at least the equal to that of Robinson. The significance of these two pioneers of gardening on the gardening scene was fundamental and far reaching; their influence in the shaping of the remaining gardens I describe in these pages is abundantly clear.

Sir Robert Lorimer the creator of the old garden at Kellie Castle and architect of many notable, and noble buildings across Scotland, would have been viewed with the gravest suspicion by William Robinson. Yet, although his gardening conceptions were coloured by an architect's craving for order and he was certainly no plantsman, nevertheless his approach was, if not revolutionary (although some say that it was), certainly distinctly advanced. And his creed that a garden must be a place of repose and solitude – a sanctuary – was in keeping with the thoughts and aims of some of the greatest gardeners through history. He succeeded in his design at his great country-house achievement at Earlshall in Fife, and also, on a smaller scale at Kellie Castle 25 kilometres away. Kellie was to be his home for a number of years, and it is now lived in by his son, the well-known sculptor, Hew Lorimer, who offered Kellie Castle to the National Trust for Scotland in 1970. But it is Sir Robert's concept of garden design which the Trust are recreating at Kellie Castle.

In 1899 R. S. Lorimer, as he then was, wrote in the *Architectural Review* an article on Scottish Gardens in which he explained what, to him, was the essence of garden design. That what he wanted was 'a garden that is in tune with the house, a garden that has a quite different sort of charm from the park outside, a garden that is an intentional and deliberate piece of careful design, a place that is garnished and nurtured with the tenderest care, but which becomes less trim as it gets further from the house, and then naturally and gradually marries with the demesne that lies beyond' – in effect the 'Wild Garden'. The approach was to be arrow straight and, ideally, there should be park on one side up to the very house walls and on the other 'you can stroll right out into the garden inclosed (as indeed happens at Kellie); but what a paradise can such a place be made! Such surprises – little gardens within the garden, the month's garden, the herb garden, the yew alley. The kitchen garden too, and this nothing to be ashamed of, to be smothered away far from the house, but made delightful by its laying out. Great intersecting walks of shaven grass, on either side borders of the brightest flowers backed up by low espaliers hanging with shining apples.' Not for Lorimer that 'arch-abomination', the specimen tree, nor the 'degraded garden', tucked into an out of the way corner a kilometre from the house.

Here we see the architect's interpretation of what was to become Gertrude Jekyll's modern garden design; and Lorimer's 'month's' garden was pure Jekyll. How too that lady would have approved of Sir Robert Lorimer's final remarks: 'But, provided the architect has sufficient tact not to try to teach the nurseryman his own business, he will very soon recognise him . . . as his friend, and come to see that the only way to arrive at a successful garden scheme, large or small, is for the two to work into each other's hands.' It was a concept she brought to triumphal achievement in her famous partnership with the architect, Edwin Lutyens, in the early 1900s and after.

How very similar this was to the precepts of Reginald Farrer, best and usually solely, associated with his rock garden work, and who wrote in 1907 in *My Rock Garden,* that 'The garden proper, as seen from the house, is a part of the house, neither more nor less than the frame is part of the picture. From which it follows that the garden must be built on calm, firm lines – either straight, or intelligibly, strongly curved. It must have a definite scheme, coherence, unity – not be a mere reckless jumble of features. It must also make one individuality with the house it belongs to, harmonise with it, continue its plan, and carry out its intention.'

Kellie Castle: in the Yew Bosquet.

It was in 1875 or 1876, that Professor James Lorimer, then Professor of Public and International Law in Edinburgh, father of Sir Robert and grandfather of the last owner, first laid eyes on Kellie. For a number of years, he and his family had been accustomed to cross the Firth of Forth for their holidays, and in the area known as the East Neuk of Fife the professor found the climate particularly suited to his asthma from which he had long suffered. On one such holiday the family penetrated inland, and there, a few kilometres from the coast and the small town of Pittenweem, they came across the crumbling old remains of Kellie Castle, gaunt and nearly derelict in the middle of a turnip field.

The professor and his wife immediately fell in love with the old place. Terms were arranged and soon afterwards the Lorimers started the seemingly endless task of restoration.

Kellie Castle dates from the twelfth or thirteenth century. For over a hundred years the House of Siward occupied the estate, then for a further two hundred that of the Oliphants; Until, in 1613, the then 5th Lord Oliphant sold castle and estate to Thomas Erskine, Viscount Fentoun, who six years later was created 1st Earl of Kellie. For more than two centuries the Earls of Kellie reigned in the castle. They were a ubiquitous family of considerable eminence in the Scotland of their day. The 3rd Earl, a Cavalier of renown and firm supporter of King Charles II, was taken at the Battle of Worcester and exiled to Holland where he married. In 1661, he and his bride returned to Kellie to find that the castle 'had been repaired by his sisters a litell before their coming' – some of the work being attributed to Sir William Bruce, the great seventeenth-century Scottish architect and garden designer, who then lived at Balcaskie five kilometres away. It was the 3rd Earl who was responsible for much of the present shape of the castle. The 5th Earl fought for Bonnie Prince Charlie as a colonel in the Jacobite army. The 6th Earl, 'Fiddler Tam', was a noted violinist and composer – his music especially distinguished by its 'loudness, rapidity and enthusiasm'. This endearing character evidently had other enthusiasms for he was known for his 'coarse joviality' and was reputed to have a countenance which 'could ripen a cucumber'! From his death the title continued in erratic line until the passing, in 1829, of the 10th Earl of Kellie, when the title was taken by the Earls of Mar.

It was then that took place the 'muckle roup', the famous auction of Kellie, which was an event of high importance in the district. Everything was sold, family pictures, tapestries, carpets, the lot. Some were salvaged and bought by the Anstruthers, then the owners of Bruce's former house at Balcaskie, but most were scattered to the winds.

And with the 'muckle roup' the old castle, now neglected and largely unlived in, started to deteriorate and decay. At one time the manager of a local coalpit lived in a few rooms with his family; at another some labourers set up their quarters. By the time Professor Lorimer fell in love with Kellie, the place was near-derelict.

Every pane of glass was broken. The roof showed daylight in a hundred places and let in rain, snow and damp. Owls and rooks had made their nests at first in the chimneys but as they crumbled beneath them, in the very rooms themselves. Floors and ceilings sagged. Weeds grew undisturbed on the walls and on the floor boards. Trees had seeded in the cracks of the masonry threatening to bring down the very walls. The garden was a wilderness through which the remains of a few roses and fruit bushes struggled to find light. Gnarled old apple trees vied for existence with a creeping jungle of ivy and bramble. Not without justification did the professor have inscribed above his door:

HOC DOMICILIUM CORVIS ET BUBONIBUS EREPTUM
HONESTO INTER LABORES OTIO CONSECRATUM EST

(This dwelling snatched from rooks and owls is dedicated to honest ease in the midst of labours)

On a clear day, from the south windows of Kellie Castle, the view is magnificent. Out to sea the Bass Rock, one of the last of the Royalist strongholds to surrender in the Civil War, looms from the water. Further towards the open sea, the sheer basaltic cliffs of the Isle of May, 10 kilometres away are just visible. On the opposite shore of the Firth one can see the chain of towns and one-time little harbours, which are the outskirts of Edinburgh itself. But on a misty day, when the ha'ar creeps in from the sea, it is impossible sometimes to see the end of the garden.

The climate is mild – the sea air sees to that – but frosts can be severe and snow lies heavy in most winters. But it is the wind that is the true gardener's curse, for at Kellie it enters the Walled Garden and swirls around unhindered.

James Lorimer set about restoring the seventeenth century enclosed garden, which must have been a feature of the old Kellie. But when Sir Robert succeeded to the place on his father's death, he determined to replace this with a Victorian garden, the feature of which was a fine selection of old roses. It is a Victorian garden, again with an emphasis on roses, that the National Trust for Scotland are establishing at Kellie Castle.

I Falkland Palace A General View of the Loaning from the Water Garden

Not until one is nearing Kellie through the avenue on the front drive can one see the castle. The first impression is of a secret castle, nestling in a mantle of fine trees and seeking only solitude. One is struck by the warmth and calm of the place: for there is nothing sinister about Kellie. Even the raucous cawing from the rookery does not seem to disturb, in fact it heightens the feeling of seclusion and peace.

A gate to the right of the castle leads through an outside garden to the main wall. Here are a number of vines and veteran fruit trees, as well as a recent planting of climbing and rambler roses, struggling to become established, for this is an exposed position. Here, amongst others, are the rampant 'Allen's Fragrant Pillar', a climbing Hybrid Tea introduced in the early 1930s a glow of flame in summer; 'Paul's Lemon Pillar' a 1915 introduction and still one of the best in its colour range of white with an ivory suffusion; the old favourites and true Victorian roses 'Climbing Caroline Testout' and the ever-popular Bourbon. 'Zéphrine Drouhin', a thornless rose; and the perpetual-flowering 'William Allen Richardson', an apricot-coloured Noisette, producing huge clusters of flowers, but really needing a warm wall to do its best.

But within the wall, is a Victorian garden in a modern guise. For Kellie is a compact garden: within the old walls, which are as old as the castle itself and which were in a terrible state of disrepair before extensive rebuilding and repointing took place, it occupies an area no more than a hectare in extent. The Castle itself provides nearly half the southern wall, and you can indeed 'stroll right out into the garden inclosed', as Lorimer invited.

The design is simple: a rectangle with criss-cross paths, each junction marked with either pillars of roses or, in one case, a fine sundial. In winter the whole garden can be taken in at a glance, but in summer it is ablaze with colour, each feature unerringly leading the visitor on to the next delight.

In the south-east corner is a yew bosquet, a secret garden with two pillars of rose and honeysuckle – a most effective combination – and a stone vase of carved basketwork, the work of Hew Lorimer. It is bordered at the back by the rose 'Six Hills' and a large bed of the herbaceous senecio, *Ligularia dentata (Senecio clivorum)* whose dark, shiny-green leaves act as a fine foil to the mellowed, litchen-covered stone of the vase.

In the opposite corner, is a new planting; a trellis-surrounded arbour, a place of repose and seclusion. Old-fashioned roses predominate here: the Damasks are represented by 'Léda', the 'Painted Damask' with luxuriant dark green foliage; the Bourbons by 'Louise Odier', a vigorous two-metre rose with a profusion of huge rich pink flowers; the Centifolias by another pink, 'La Noblesse', which has the inestimable advantage of continuing the centifolia season well into late summer; and the Albas by that old favourite 'Königin von Danemarck'. These are underplanted with a skilful mixture of eryngiums, cat-mint and *Linum narbonense,* whose grey lanceolate leaves are a perfect foil to their rich blue flowers. At the rear, is a thin herbaceous border linking with the trellis which is to be planted with clematis and other climbers. The whole, particularly in that setting, should make a most effective planting.

From here, the visitor inevitably walks down the garden with the wide, perfectly-tended vegetable borders on the one side, backed by equally well-trained fruit trees – British kitchen-garden planting at its best. On the other side the path is flanked by long, narrow borders of mixed herbaceous subjects and shrubs – viburnums, philadelphus, deutzias, the grey-leaved hybrid *Buddleia* 'Lochinch', the purple-leaved diervilla, *Weigela florida* 'Foliis Purpureis', and many others. Halfway down the main walk is a colossal tree of *Garrya elliptica,* one of David Douglas' great finds. This specimen is all of six metres high and as many across and is clearly only a sapling of what must have been a tremendous tree indeed. It is a magnificent sight in January and February with its huge catkins, 10, 13, even 15cm. long against its rich evergreen foliage.

And now we come upon more roses; a rose rampart, cut at shoulder-height and rigorously trained, of the famous Alba, 'Celestial', whose beautiful pointed pink buds are one of the greatest delights in the rose family. These open to transparent pink, rather delicate flowers 12cm. across, the whole set against a soft grey-green foliage which is a delight in itself. Elsewhere there are other rose hedges, one of the striped rose 'Rosa Mundi' (*Rosa gallica* 'Versicolor') and another of the robust and willing 'Fellemberg', an almost continuous flowerer from early June until the frosts come.

In the side borders are other shrubs: a huge *Exochorda macrantha,* covered with racemes of large white flowers in May and June, and an equally-large *Rosa moyesii.*

But it is the main borders which are the chief attraction of Kellie and run the length of the garden. For the most part they consist of perennial herbaceous plants; annuals too are extensively used and also a number of shrubby subjects including some fine tree peonies. The rose garlands at the back of the borders are a principal feature. Swathed in chains, here are the old favourites of our Victorian ancestors and some of a more recent origin: 'American Pillar', 'Albertine', (1921) and 'Dorothy Perkins'. The curiously named 'Rambling Rector' scrambles up one old apple tree, and up wire arches we find 'Dorothy Perkins' and 'American Pillar' again – neither everyone's modern choice for a rose, but in this setting singularly appropriate. Each year those tied to metal supports are badly frosted, but each year, after this initial check, they seem to thrive the more.

In some of the borders are clematis trained up pyramidal supports, including 'Perle d'Azur', 'Jackmanii Superba', the excellent lavender 'Belle Nantaise' and the huge mauve-pink 'Comtesse de Bouchard'.

In one corner of the garden is a charming stone cottage with a hen carved on the roof: here can be found more roses, and *Kerria japonica*. In another, close under the towering walls of the castle, a damp and shaded spot, is a planting of mauve and white astilbes and bergenias, while on the walls in this unfavourable corner is *Cotoneaster* × *watereri*, *Hydrangea petiolaris* and the Virginian Creeper. Across the path, in only a fractionally better position, are groups of solomon's seal and monkshood.

Although not very large, the Kellie Castle garden has a lot of interest. But, to me, it is the atmosphere and the situation of the place that has such compelling charm. It is not difficult to understand how Professor Lorimer and his wife came to fall in love with the old castle so many years ago.

How to get there

4 km north of PITTENWEEM; 80 km EDINBURGH
Turn off east at Exit 3 on EDINBURGH-PERTH Motorway (M90) on to *A910* to KIRKCALDY – then *A915* to KIRKTON OF LARGO – right on *A921*

SEVEN

Crathes Castle *Kincardineshire*

THE CLIMATE on the east coast of Scotland is far less amenable than that on the west coast: a lower rainfall – 80 cm. (32in.) a year on average – combined with severe frosts – –18°C (0°F) has been known at times – and often heavy snow, which can linger for weeks, if not indeed months. For there is no warming breeze from the south-west; instead, a searing, icy easterly blast, comes seemingly straight from the Steppes of Russia, and will cut back precocious growth as though with a blow-torch. No gardener would consider this part of Scotland a particularly favourable climate for plants, but at Crathes Castle – probably the best known Scottish garden in the north-east of the country – is an outstanding collection of shrubs and other plants, many of which are considered only doubtfully hardy, in even the most favoured parts of the country.

The Burnett of Leys are among the very few Scottish families who can claim descent from an English ancestor of Saxon times. The Burnards – a Bedfordshire family – first gain mention in the Scottish history books when Alexander Burnard accompanied David I on his return to Scotland to claim his kingdom in the twelfth century. Throughout the national struggles that succeeded this event, Burnard stood staunchly by, and, as his reward, was granted land, firstly in the Border country, then by Robert the Bruce, who was helped by a Burnard in a later century, in the Royal Forest of Drum on Deeside. The horn of Leys, reputedly presented by Robert the Bruce, is preserved in the Castle.

The royal gift included what was then the Loch and Island of Banchory, the now drained Loch of Leys. It was on this island that the Burnards made their home until, with the coming of the sixteenth century, less disturbed times enabled the Burnetts, as they had by then become, to move to more congenial surroundings and a more commodious and accessible site. They chose that at Crathes some three kilometres from their island home, where a gentle south-facing slope afforded a pleasant view over the hills of Deeside, and the Hill of Fare gave some protection from the north. Work on Crathes commenced around 1553, but owing to various interruptions in the uneasy political climate of the time, not until 1594 was the Burnett of the day able to move into his new home, and it was far from complete even then.

The style of building, in the construction of which the Scots became such masters, with its small roofspace and emphasis on height, was in part dictated by the defensive needs of the time, in part by an acute shortage of timber. When Crathes came to be built, the Forest of Drum had long since disappeared; the little oak that remained was reserved for those parts of the building for which no adequate substitute could be found – the heavy outer doors and, as at Crathes, roofing for the long gallery (a rare feature in Scottish houses). Wood for roof and floors was imported from the Baltic and Scandinavia, and whenever possible the use of timber was dispensed with altogether; at Crathes the first two floors were constructed without using any timber at all.

As the visitor rounds the last bend on the long approach to the Castle, he is greeted by his first glimpse of Crathes. And it is a breathtaking one. Set in flowing lawns, the fine harled* walls of the castle rise slender and without interruption to a remarkable height. But, instead of being surmounted by battlement and austere turret, the whole erupts into a wealth of corbels and bartisans, crow-steps, gargoyles and finials. The fairy castle effect is irresistible: what could be a gaunt, forbidding edifice is transformed into something of great beauty, the hard lines softened; although the needs for defence cannot have been far from the mind of the architect, he has created what above all else was a home.

As successive generations of Burnetts lived at Crathes, the castle grew and developed. Most significant of these builders was Sir Thomas Burnett, the 3rd Baronet, who, in the time of Queen Anne built a further storey to the south wing of the Castle – probably to accommodate the twenty-one children his wife bore him in

* rough-cast with lime and small gravel.

twenty-three years. It is probable too, that around then the barmkin, or outer courtyard characteristic of Scottish castles, was removed. From a drab service wing, the Queen Anne wing, as it came to be called, became the most elegant feature of the house. This, and another extension built in the nineteenth century, were burnt to the ground in a disastrous fire in 1966. Thus, by chance, the existing building looks much as it did when it was first built over four hundred years ago.

There is no record of how the old garden at Crathes may have looked. Only the superb lime avenue, which marked the line of the old carriage drive, and the wonderful yew hedges, both planted by the 3rd Baronet around the turn of the eighteenth century, survive. There is also a Portugal Laurel (*Prunus lusitanica*) cut in the shape of a giant toadstool, which is said to date from that period. All of which leads one to think that a strictly formal style of garden existed then. We do know, however, that in 1714 the garden was reputed to 'produce delicate fruit; the soil is warm, the victuals substantial and weighty'. And that, at a later date, the vineries at Crathes were renowned throughout the district.

By the time Major-General Sir James and Lady Burnett of Leys came to live at Crathes in 1926, Sir James had been a shrub enthusiast for a number of years. His was the enthusiasm of a collector. The difficulty in growing the plants he chose was the challenge, the overcoming of it the satisfaction – and he planted his shrubs all over the garden. It was to impart some sort of order to this haphazard planting, that Lady Burnett, who had known little of gardening before, turned her hand to the garden at Crathes. Immediately, her natural flair for planting the right things in the right place, for great imagination and a true artist's touch became vividly apparent. Herbaceous planting was her forte – and she had few rivals.

Thus, the garden at Crathes, as we know it today, is the achievement of two people: one a highly knowledgeable shrub connoisseur, the other no less an authority on herbaceous plants, with a flair for grouping and mass effect. But the achievement was not without its little frictions, as could only be expected with two such strong personalities. When, as happened from time to time, a desirable piece of ground became vacant, or some plant had succumbed to the North-East Scottish climate, the in-fighting became fierce. First on the scene might be Sir James ready to earmark the spot for some highly-desirable shrub; to be followed, not long after, by Lady Burnett with equally determined plans of quite a different nature. MacDonald, the head gardener, who still after many years, lovingly maintains the Crathes tradition and perpetuates the atmosphere which the Burnetts did so much to create, would listen and . . . do nothing – safe in the knowledge that this was merely a preliminary skirmish in a long-drawn-out engagement. After weeks of behind-the-scenes diplomacy, tact and a persistence which did credit to both protagonists, would come the day of decision. Perhaps, this time, her Ladyship would get her way, but only, to be sure, at the cost of some equally desirable bit of real estate. The result is a perfect harmony: of the garden with the old castle; of herbaceous plants, with a plantsman's collection of rare shrubs; of garden effect, with a botanist's eye for detail.

Not without justification is Crathes likened to Hidcote. Not just because it is a beautiful garden, but also because the styles are similar. However, whereas at Hidcote, Lawrence Johnston elected to create his formal setting, the Burnetts at Crathes, as indeed did the Nicholsons at Sissinghurst, found themselves with a natural inheritance, which largely dictated the resulting overall style of gardening.

The first glimpse one gets of the garden is from the wide grassy plateau on which the Castle stands. From here the ground falls gently to the south and east, and it is on the broad south-east slope, in a good medium loam, that the famous gardens have been developed. Below, are the black masses of the magnificent yew hedges, rightly the pride of Crathes, which create the framework for the upper gardens. Fully three metres high, and as many across, they are over 250 years old. Immaculately trimmed and shaped – a task which used to occupy three men the year round – they provide the perfect backdrop and the formal surrounds to the imaginative planting in what must be one of the most beautiful gardens in these islands.

From the Castle entrance it is only a few paces to the top of the Upper Terrace. Through an arch formed by a couple of Irish yews of considerable antiquity, steps lead down to what is known as the Croquet Lawn and the Pool Garden, where once was an oak and a peach house, one of the first things Lady Burnett was to do away with at Crathes. Started in 1932, the Pool Garden was the last of

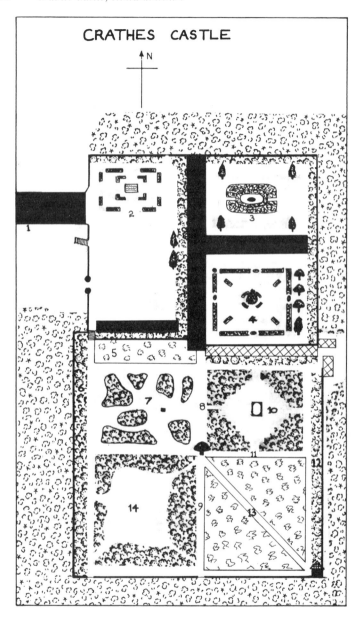

CRATHES CASTLE

N

1. Crathes Castle
2. Pool Garden
3. Fountain Garden
4. Rose Garden
5. Aviary Border
6. West Herbaceous Border
7. Camel Garden
8. Double Herbaceous Border
9. Double Shrub Border
10. Trough & Garden
11. White Border
12. Dovecote Border
13. June Border
14. Yellow Garden

Lady Burnett's achievements. The colour scheme in the broad border on the west-facing wall is red, purple and yellow, and immensely effective it is. Conspicuous in this border is the red *Papaver commutatum*; the deep purple of *Cotinus coggygria* 'Foliis Purpureis', the purple form of the Burning Bush, and the clear yellow daisies of *Coreopsis verticillata,* which has a satisfactorily prolonged flowering season. Here too can be found *Berberis thunbergii* 'Atropurpurea' and the purple sage, *Salvia officinalis* 'Purpurescens'. Against the wall are a number of interesting climbers, and two honeysuckles, *Lonicera splendida,* from Spain, a really beautiful climber with glaucous leaves, and the highly decorative *L. tragophylla* from Western China, which does best in complete shade. Also can be seen a huge *Schizophragma integrifolia;* the yellow clematis, *C. tangutica;* and *Azara lanceolata*; also a number of roses which are too rarely seen in gardens today: old 'Veilchenblau', an early flowering crimson-purple rambler; 'Easlea's Golden Rambler', with very un-rambler-like rich yellow flowers and a glossy green foliage, and 'William Allen Richardson', a rose produced as far back as 1878 with great clusters of apricot flowers. In the corner by the Castle are other interesting plants: an unusual cross-bred garrya, *G.* × *thuretii,* and a fascinating and charming bramble, *Rubus ulmifolius* 'Bellidiflorus', with double pink flowers, a very showy variety but a rampant grower.

The pond area is formally planted, with clipped yew hedges and fastigiate junipers. Four 'L'-shaped beds are devoted to shrubs and roses, including 'Blanc Double de Coubert', and the purple 'Cardinal de Richelieu'.

Across the lawn are specimen hollies, yews and privet interspersed with the architectural *Kniphofia caulescens,* a huge, grey-leaved Red Hot Poker. Two venerable specimens of the Irish yew stand guard over the steps which lead to the lower levels and to the yew borders. Here is a different world, a place of cool walks and half-shade and a piece of the garden protected from the wind. Here the plantsman can appreciate to the full how extensive was the collection of trees and shrubs made by Sir James Burnett.

The steps are wreathed in *Clematis macropetala,* but almost the first plant to strike the eye is *Cornus nuttallii,* whose large white bracts produced in May make it perhaps the most striking of the dogwoods. Not far away is *Dipelta floribunda* whose weigela-like flowers are also produced in May. *Jamesia americana* is a small shrub related to the deutzias, with greyish leaves and 1cm. fragrant white flowers. Here too can be found a specimen of *Sophora japonica,* the Japanese Pagoda Tree; *Koelreuteria paniculata,* the Goldenrain Tree, with useful yellow flowers in July and August; *Staphylea colchica,* another May-flowerer, and *Eucryphia glutinosa,* the only one of the genus which will flower well at Crathes, and many, many more climbers, trees and other shrubs.

Within the two enclosures formed by the Yew Borders are two other gardens – the Fountain Garden and the Rose Garden. The Fountain Garden, a formal garden in the Victorian mould, with its lovely background of the vast yew hedges, is dominated by the replica of a Florentine statue, which is surrounded by box-edged beds. The prevailing colour is blue, supplied by the invaluable *Echium* 'Blue Bedder', cornflowers, and *Asperula orientalis (azurea setosa),* with *Agapanthus orientalis* in ornamental stone vases. The result is simple, cool and effective.

The rose garden is dominated by a splendid *Stranvaesia davidiana,* in the centre bed; the geometrically-shaped beds around are planted with Floribunda roses, of which the most noteworthy is the ever-popular, almost luminescent 'Iceberg'. The rose border on the west of the Rose Garden is full of old-fashioned and species roses: *Rosa moyesii,* 'Sealing Wax', a vastly better coloured rose than the type; *R. nitida*; *R. webbiana,* a West Himalayan species, with huge pink flowers carried all along the stem and sealing-wax fruits in the autumn; the lovely modern shrub roses 'Fritz Nobis' and 'Golden Wings'; the Rugosa 'Roserai de l'Haÿ'; and the incomparable, almost continuous-flowering Alba 'Souvenir de la Malmaison'.

Around the Fountain and the Rose Garden are wide borders against the high Crathes wall. Here are further examples of Sir James' magnificent shrubs, many of them from the Far East, where he had served and travelled widely in his army days. In one corner is a near-relation of the rose, *Prinsepia utilis,* a spring-flowerer from the Himalayas; nearby is *Rosa gigantea,* a species from Burma, with 5-7cm white flowers and bright red hips, and another rose, a hybrid *R. spinosissima,* 'Stanwell Perpetual', a charming pink rose which, surprisingly, is almost perpetually flowering. An unusual buddleia can be found here, *Buddleia tibetica,* with lilac panicles in spring; an equally unusual weigela, *Weigela middendorffiana,* with yellow flowers and a good, compact growth, a shrub with a lot of potential; and a group of enormous *Aralia elata* 'Variegata', ('Albo-marginata'), a stupendous sight in a corner against the great yew hedges, which was one of Lady Burnett's especial favourites, and it is not hard to see why.

Beyond is a terrace overlooking the lower garden. And perhaps it was there that one day under the huge *Eucalyptus gunnii* Sir James was accosted by two ladies who asked him what was the name of a certain plant.

'Meconopsis', was the brief reply.

'And where do they come from, Sir James?'

'Himalayas.'

'Oh thank you so much, Sir James. We shall write to them as soon as we get home!'

Crathes: The Fountain Garden.

The Lower Garden is divided into separate compartments, divided by transverse paths. On the right is the Camel Garden – so called from the two raised beds in the middle – and the newly created Yellow Garden; to the left is the Trough Garden and behind is what is currently a nursery. Between the four, radiating from the central toadstool Portugal Laurel, lie Lady Burnett's greatest achievements – the White Border, the Double Herbaceous Border and the June

Border, which runs diagonally towards an attractive 17th century stone Doocot (or Dovecote) which was moved to its present site in 1937.

Best known, and rightly so, is the White Border. Here, against a background of the purple plum, *Prunus cerasifera* 'Pissardii' ('Atropurpurea') which is kept 1.8 metres high by vigorous pruning and amid a medley of white herbaceous plants, silver foliage and low-growing shrubs and Shrub Roses chosen as much for their scent as for their colour, is a perfect example of the art of mixed border planting at its very best. Fifty-five metres long and nearly two metres wide, the clever use of colour, and texture and tone and height is fascinating. Conspicuous is the great Donkey Fart Thistle, *Onopordon acanthium,* growing up to 2.5 metres high; almost as tall is *Echinops humilis* with blue spheres and 'cobweb-covered' dark green leaves – for this is not a wholly white border. *Salix lanata,* with silvery leaves, is a case in point, and even *Philadelphus* 'Belle Etoile', or *Hydrangea peniculata* 'Grandiflora', when out of season provides a restful contrast with glaring white. But white there is in plenty, from Rose 'Wedding Day', *Stachys lanata, Artemisia ludoviciana,* white phlox and white delphiniums, *Cimicifuga racemosa* and others. At the front *Anaphalis triplinervis* has been widely planted.

The other borders radiating from the Portugal laurel are of equal fascination and worthy of study, particularly the June border with its backing of *Prunus* 'Amanogawa'.

The Camel Garden with several island-beds is crammed with interesting shrubs and herbaceous plants designed to give colour, and contrast the year through. An object lesson on how to treat a small area and provide a continuing interest. On the western side on a trellis and beyond on the wall, there grow a number of roses and other climbers including, two rubus, *R. ulmifolius* 'Bellidiflorus', again, and *R. phoeniculasius,* the Wineberry, with red bristly stems and delicious fruits. Some of the roses are of particular merit the Rugosa 'Agnes', with double flowers of a rich apricot colour, it has two flowering periods; *R. soulieana,* with large white clusters of flowers and lovely glaucous stems; and the underrated and very vigorous 'Lawrence Johnston', which is named after the creator of Hidcote. Raised in 1923, this rose languished unappreciated for many years, only receiving an Award of Merit from the Royal Horticultural Society in 1948. Of a gloriously warm, rich yellow, with a powerful scent and an excellent 'doer', it features in too few gardens, and too few rose catalogues.

But my personal favourite of what Sir Robert Lorimer called his gardens within a garden, is the Trough Garden. In the centre of a small lawn, a colossal mahogany-barked *Prunus serrula* overhangs a large stone trough, to create a picture almost Japanese in its simplicity. Around are beds with skilfully curved edges in which are superbly grown, and cleverly chosen, trees and shrubs and other plants, which provide colour for many months and interest throughout the year. In spring and early summer *Trillium grandiflorum*, *Berberis linearifolia* and various pulmonarias will attract attention, and one bed has a selection of lilacs, including the species *Syringa* × *persica*, *S. sweginzowii* and the graceful *S. julianae*, as well as a number of cultivars including the double white 'Madame Lemoine' and the yellow 'Primrose'. Two snowdrop trees, *Halesia monticola vestita* and *H. carolina*, are at their best in May. In the autumn, colour comes from *Fothergilla monticola* with a clever underplanting of *Sedum* 'Autumn Joy' and *Gentiana sino-ornata* as well as a number of acers, including the lovely flaking-bark maple *Acer griseum*; as well as many other shrubs and trees.

Returning towards the Castle again, a small garden with a collection of grasses will catch the eye. As will the Enkianthus Walk, a path lined on both sides with *Enkianthus* species, *EE. campanulatus tectus*, *perulatus*, *campanulatus recurvus* and *cernuus*. It is a matter for debate whether these look best in May when the enkianthus is in full blossom, against the underplanting of blue viola, or in the autumn when the enkianthus bursts into its unrivalled autumn colouring.

Around the boundary walls of the Lower Garden are yet more fascinating and not a few highly unusual and semi-hardy shrubs. Particularly noteworthy is the salmon-flowered *Phygelius aequalis*, more tender than its near relation the Cape Figwort. In this corner by a flight of stone steps is a charming little planting of *Actinidia kolomikta*, the phygelius, *Chimonanthus praecox* and *Hebe pinguifolia* 'Pagei'.

Outside the walled garden, hardly noticed and rarely visited, is a small pond, an oasis surrounded by willow and aralia, berberis and the superb white-leaved *Sorbus aria 'Lutescens'*. This little garden is a surprise and a delight.

No mere words can do justice to the delights of Crathes. The contrast between the light-coloured Castle and the dark yew hedges creates an incomparable setting, and the way this has been exploited is a continuing and developing fascination. Nowhere does sheer magnificence overwhelm. The borders, superb in form, in colour and in plant association, are still small enough for each subtlety of planting to be enjoyed. For the plantsman, there is a never-ending succession of delights; for the garden designer, there is a life-time's education; for the casual visitor, there is the chance to marvel at what is undoubtedly one of the finest gardens in the country. If such a thing as a perfect garden exists, Crathes must come very near to that perfection.

How to get there

26 km west of ABERDEEN; 5 km east of BANCHORY
A93 west from ABERDEEN

EIGHT

Brodick   *Isle of Arran*

SET ON AN eminence fifty metres above the shores of the Firth of Clyde, and guarding the vulnerable approaches to Western Scotland, stands Brodick Castle on the Isle of Arran. From here, a magnificent panorama meets the eye; of the wide sweep of the Firth, of the coast of Ayrshire, of Troon, of the city of Ayr (19 kilometres north of Culzean) and the soft hills of Kyle, beyond. Given complete protection from the prevailing west and south-west winds, basking in the warmth of the North Atlantic Drift, product of the distant Gulf Stream, Brodick is home to a wealth of unusual and semi-tender plants. A true west-coast paradise.

The visitor will arrive by boat, probably by ferry from the little port of Ardrossan. As the Isle of Arran comes into view, and the spine of spectacular peaks which runs the length of the island becomes more than a distant, shadowy outline, a thickly-wooded valley will be seen in the lea of the highest of these hills, Goatfell. In these trees, well above the shore line, the observant will notice a grassy plateau and on this he should be able to pick out a red-brick, castellated mansion – Brodick Castle.

The Isle of Arran, in its important strategic position, has long been a source of squabble. From earliest time, as one wave of Celtic and other invaders followed another on the west coast of Scotland, Arran has been in the forefront of affairs. Relics of past ages bear witness to this importance – from those of the shellfish-eating mesolithic people, to the stone circles and standing-stones of Bronze Age settlement. From the ninth century AD, however, it was the Vikings who were undisputed masters of Arran, and it was they who first developed the immensely strong natural position and built a fort near or on the present site of Brodick Castle. By the twelfth century, the hardy Norsemen had yielded control of Arran and much of western Scotland to the romantically-named King of the Isles, ancestor to the MacDonalds Lords of the Isles of a more modern era.

The year 1307 found Robert the Bruce collecting his forces at Brodick for his liberation of Scotland, which ended, seven years later with his triumph over the English at the memorable Battle of Bannockburn. For much of the succeeding centuries, Brodick was a royal property, but in 1503, the long connection with the Hamilton family was begun – a connection only broken, in 1958, when Brodick Castle passed into the hands of the National Trust for Scotland.

Sheltered from the torments of the south-west gales, which are so common on this coast in winter, Brodick lies protected in a fold of the hills. The chief enemy is the spring frosts, more often than not accompanied by a chilling easterly wind, and this combination can wreak havoc – particularly if the wood of the previous year was not thoroughly ripened. Mists and dull days are rare and there is no shortage of rain – 120cm. (68in.) on average – but somehow this never seems too much. The soil is a good loam on the higher ground and generations of accumulated leaf-mould create wonderful conditions for woodland plants – although Brodick's latitude can prove a handicap to those plants needing high light intensities to do well. Sometimes shade-lovers thrive better in more open positions. From place to place in the garden, great outcrops of the indigenous red sandstone erupt to create dells and crannies, where complete protection and the perfect settings may be found for the wealth of plants of all sorts which relish the lush air of Brodick.

On a gate into the lovely old walled-garden at Brodick appears the date 1710, and doubtless a garden of sorts must have existed then; but of this there is no record and, apart from the walls, no trace remains today.

When the late Duchess of Montrose came to live at Brodick, shortly after the First World War, below the Castle and along the lip of ancient raised-beach which marked the water-level in some previous millenium, an almost impenetrable jungle of *Rhododendron ponticum* reigned undisturbed. Here and there, towering over the undergrowth, but with the full majesty of their trunks obscured, could be seen some fine trees of Silver Fir and Scots Pine, some oaks and sycamore. But the whole area was by now a primitive tangle, the

III Kellie Castle The Walled Garden

IV Brodick Castle Inside the Walled Garden

Brodick: Cordyline indivisa.

bushes growing over the few walks that survived had to be pruned hard back annually before even the paths became overgrown and lost forever.

One day in the early 1920s, the Duchess was presented with a box of primulas, and, wanting to see them happily established, she started to have cleared a space along a narrow ditch. Once begun, the process continued. At first small bays, and then larger areas were cleared among the ponticums. It was while this was in progress that she was accosted by an old gardener who declared 'I dinna think we should dae that, there's a hydro in there, and Mr Inglis (the forester) might no be pleased.' As the Duchess said later, 'I could not imagine from this reply what had been found in the bushes and did not like to show my ignorance'. But investigation ensued, and to her considerable astonishment a magnificent hybrid rhododendron came to light. And other trees of a previous planting were found as the clearing continued. Thus began the garden we know today at Brodick Castle, a garden of international repute, and one of never-ending delight to visitors.

Gifts of seedlings, of rhododendrons, primulas and many other plants came from the Royal Botanic Garden at Edinburgh, from

Ardgowan and Stonefield, both west-coast gardens of note, and from the Montrose's many other friends. Then, in 1930, the Montrose's elder daughter married Major John Boscawen, nephew of Colonel Dorrien-Smith of that great garden at Tresco Abbey in the Scillies; and then a new era began for Brodick. The garden today is the joint achievement of two very talented gardeners.

Not many months after the wedding, a puffer, the small local coastal steamer, sailed asthmatically into Brodick Bay, laden with trees, shrubs, bushes and bulbs from Tresco. These provided the foundation for the quite remarkable collection of semi-tender plants at Brodick. For, curiously enough, the winter isotherm of 5°C (40°F) runs through both Arran and the Scillies.

The Duchess of Montrose's enthusiasm for gardening could not have been better-timed. This was the second golden age of plant-hunters. The collections of Kingdon-Ward, Rock, Farrer and many others were flooding the country. To many of these expeditions the owner of Brodick subscribed, and many of the incomparable discoveries found their way back to Brodick. But of all the great collectors of this period a Scotsman, George Forrest, was king, and it is with Forrest that Brodick is most closely associated.

A small, stocky Scotsman, with a constitution of iron, Forrest was born at Falkirk in 1873. His initial botanical training was as a chemist, but he soon tired of that, and a fortunate legacy found him the means to go to Australia where he worked as gold prospector, lumberjack and sheep farmer. Wearying of Australia, he returned to Scotland and, so the story goes, one day he was sheltering from a shower of rain and noticed a peculiar slab of stone sticking out from a shingly bank. This turned out to be an ancient stone coffin with the remains of a skeleton inside. In the course of following up this discovery Forrest came to Professor Bailey Balfour, Regius Keeper of the Edinburgh Botanic Gardens. Whether this story is true or apochryphal, has never been determined, but certainly near the turn of the century Forrest was working at the Botanic Gardens. And, when A. K. Bulley, founder of the famous seed firm of Bees Ltd, was seeking a professional plant collector to tap the wealth of plants which missionaries had shown to exist in China, Balfour had no hesitation in recommending Forrest. So began one of the greatest partnerships in the history of gardening, a partnership which in 20 years produced over 31,000 plants, almost all new to our gardens, and many new to science – a mind-boggling total which has never been exceeded, and never will be.

In 1902, Forrest set out on the first of his seven great trips to that piece of country which lies near the borders of China, Tibet and Burma. For seventeen years he was plant collecting in that virtually unknown and inhospitable region, fighting disease, hardship and danger. Sadly he died in 1932 on what was to have been his last trip. At first, knowing no Chinese, he met opposition and suspicion at every turn, but the imperturbality and kindness of this tough little Scotsman won him friends. By the end, through his own dedication and effort, he had a team of highly-trained and responsible assistants able to work on their own, in their master's rare absences. Even after Forrest's death; Lord Aberconway was able to employ some of Forrest's men.

As the volume of Forrest's finds so diligently collected in the field found their way back to Edinburgh, so Balfour, and after him his successor Sir William Wright-Smith, catalogued and classified with corresponding diligence. And what of Forrest's finds: of rhododendrons – 309 species new to science; of primulas – 154 species, including – *PP. aurantiaca, chionantha, helodoxa, beesiana, bulleyana* (both named in honour of his sponsor), *malacoides* and the beautiful *littoniana* (vialii), named after his close friend G. L. Litton who was British Consul in Tengueh, the base for many of his expeditions. And, of course, the incomparable *Gentiana sino-ornata*, described by David Wilkie, a great gentian authority as 'the finest all round garden plant to be introduced in this century'. The debt gardeners owe to Forrest is immeasurable, and not just for the species he sent back, but also for the innumerable hybrids that have resulted from his finds.

From the terrace of the Castle, the true magnificence of the position Brodick occupies can be appreciated. Behind, towers the massif of Goatfell; ahead lies the Firth of Clyde and the coast of Ayrshire; in the foreground stands the canopy of trees which provide the necessary protection for the many fine shrubs and plants for which Brodick is so famous. To the left is the Walled Garden with a number of wall shrubs topping the stonework and inviting further inspection, particularly the attractive mauve flowers of *Abutilon vitifolium*, a perfect foil against the greyish-white leaves. Down the side of the wall runs a path, and this is where the visitor is advised to make his way.

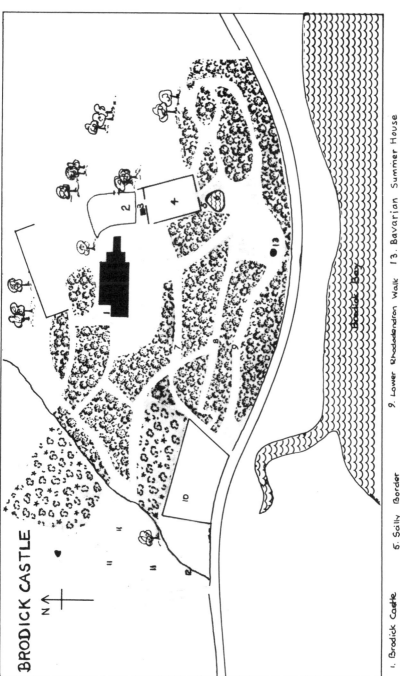

BRODICK CASTLE

N

1. Brodick Castle
2. Tennis Court Lawn
3. Summer House
5. Scilly Border
6. Pond
7. Old Drive
8. Middle Rhododendron Walk
9. Lower Rhododendron Walk
10. Kitchen Garden (private)
11. Horlick Collection
12. Mill Water Burn
13. Bavarian Summer House

Brodick Bay

First inkling that the climate and growth at Brodick is something rather special, appears almost immediately, for here, on the low boughs of a sycamore, ferns have seeded themselves profusely to give a semi-tropical effect that seems altogether appropriate. And then, ahead, is a plant of sensational appearance: this is *Echium wildpretii* (*E. bourgeanum*), a native of the Canary Islands, and, astonishingly, a biennial. With its huge greenish-grey leaves and colossal flower spikes, like massive bedposts standing 2.5m. tall, it is a plant for a lunarscape. The whole spike is a mass of pinkish-mauve tubular flowers, a sensational and awe-inspiring sight when in full flower in June.

Ahead may be seen the first of the meconopsis and primulas which grow so well at Brodick. A path leads to the left below the Walled Garden, the Scilly Border it used to be called, as here many of the plants sent from Tresco found their homes. And it is still home for a number of exciting and unusual plants. Chief among these is a Chilean, *Jovellana violacea*, a rampant grower to 1.8m. at Brodick, and spreading furiously by suckers. The dark-green 2cm. toothed leaves of this plant are almost obscured by hundreds of tiny violet calceolaria-like flowers (but without the pouch). This plant can survive in less favourable spots, even in London, but it is reputedly a shy flowerer.

Also in this border are two leptospermums, members of the myrtle family, namely *L. scoparium*, the 'Manuka' or New Zealand Tea Tree, with white flowers, and its variety *L.s.* 'Nicholsii' with pink flowers. Hereabouts, too is *Buddleia colvilei*, a Himalayan native first discovered by Hooker in 1849 – with beautiful hanging panicles of rose-coloured flowers. At first one might think the delicious fragrance around here emanates from the buddleia or from the *Clematis tangutica* which tangles on the wall behind, but soon the scent can be traced to a rhododendron with lax, floppy, white flowers. This is 'Fragrantissimum', one of the earliest of hybrids, the result of a cross, *R. edgworthii* × *formosum*, in 1868. This is an outstanding rhododendron, more normally found as a pot plant or in a greenhouse, except in Cornwall.

Hereabouts may be seen *Eucryphia cordifolia* and in a nearby birch tree, *Rosa filipes* 'Kiftsgate' has nearly reached the uppermost branches. A most effective combination are the blue potato flowers of *Solanum crispum* growing through the grey-toothed leaves of an olearia. Elsewhere in June, the bell-shaped hanging flowers of *Styrax japonica* are a striking sight, as is a tree of *Magnolia salicifolia* with fragrant white star flowers nearly 10cm. across, which has the inestimable advantage of flowering when still quite a young tree.

A small forest of *Olearia semidentata* leads one to a pond. This is a delightful spot in June, with sheets of orange candelabra primulas and a backdrop of *Gunnera manicata* and the almost-dwarfed *Iris kaempferi*. In this area can be seen a number of exciting trees and shrubs, including *Pieris formosa forrestii* – which was discovered by Forrest around 1910 and first shown at the Chelsea Show in 1924, where it created a sensation and was awarded an Award of Merit; *Halesia monticola*, the Mountain Snowdrop Tree of the south-eastern United States; and *Clethra arborea*, the 'Folhado' of Madeira, a tender evergreen subject with fragrant lily-of-the-valley flowers from August to October. Below the pond is what used to be the old Moraine garden, a place where the Duchess of Montrose kept her special treasures. When labour became impossible to find during the war years, and following the decimation of the great frosts of 1941, this was the first area to be given up. Now the ledges and pockets are largely devoted to primulas.

A new planting of ericas and dwarf rhododendrons leads to the Lower Rhododendron Walk, the home of the large-leaved rhododendrons, for which Brodick is so famous. On the way can be seen a particularly fine *Rhododendron magnificum*. Introduced by Kingdon-Ward in 1931, it would seem probable that this was a plant from the original seed: it has dense trusses of rose-coloured flowers, which form a beautiful combination against the enormous leaves which are nearly 40cm. long, with a greyish-white indumentum beneath.

But it is in the Lower Rhododendron Walk, sheltered by thick belts of ponticum and where frosts are rare, that are the prides of Brodick. Here are *R. giganteum,* appropriately the largest of known rhododendrons, and very tender. Discovered by Forrest in 1919 in the depth of Yunnan, it was there growing over 25m tall, the trunk nearly 2.5m. in girth. The leaves have been known to be up to 40cm. long, and have a reddish-brown colouring beneath; the flowers in great trusses of 20-25 blossoms are of a deep rose-crimson. The beautiful *R. macabeanum* is well represented, a shrub with 30cm. leaves and superb light yellow flowers, and of course *R. sinogrande,* one of Forrest's best known introductions, with dark, shiny green leaves, which can reach a length of 75cm., and creamy-white flowers with a reddish blotch. A later collection of this species by Kingdon Ward produced a plant unlike any rhododendron seen before, appropriately, the exciting new discovery was named *R. mollyanum,* after the great creator of Brodick, who had subscribed to this, as to many other expeditions.

Along the Lower Rhododendron Walk, is a small path leading up to the Bavarian Summer House, a charming little 'Shadowe House', built in 1845 to commemorate the marriage of the 10th Duke's eldest son to Princess Marie of Baden. The original work, including the remarkable mosaic of fir cones, reminiscent of the shell-work which was a Victorian pastime, was done by Bavarian craftsmen. When that started to fall to bits, it was restored and added to through the generosity and skill of a girls' school on the Isle of Wight – indistinguishably from the work of the original artists.

At the end of the Lower Rhododendron Walk, beyond and above the kitchen-garden with its greenhouses and propagating frames, is what is known as the Horlick Collection – a selection of plants, including many hybrid rhododendrons of his own raising, from Achamore, the late Sir James Horlick's beautiful garden on the Island of Gigha. He was unable to present the whole garden to the National Trust for Scotland, but, uniquely, he has presented its plants; it is now the intention of the Trust to gradually transfer, or duplicate, the better specimens, those of the larger varieties coming to Brodick, the smaller ones being sent to Threave Gardens in Kirkcudbrightshire.

The return path to the Middle Rhododendron Walk, leads past more rhododendrons and camellias. Towards the Castle, may be found the fine collection of the *Maddenii* series of rhododendrons, many of which are highly scented. Among others *R. taggianum,* a particular tender shrub and one of the finest of a magnificent group. Discovered and introduced by Forrest in 1925, the flowers in bud are cream, but opening to the purest white with a texture like the finest porcelain – a very beautiful plant.

And so, back to the Scilly Border, through the gate into the Walled Garden. This is in three grassed tiers, with a central path which leads to a small herbaceous garden at the bottom. Forty years ago the whole of the lower terrace was a collection of formal flower beds. It was here that the Duchess of Montrose could exercise to the full her artistry in plant selection and, with infinite care and patience, would experiment with various colour schemes, until perfection was reached. The great formal colour groupings are no more; instead – and possibly of comparable charm – is a simple, but effective bedding scheme centred on a small paved area with a sundial and surrounded by a rose pergola. The planting is neither complicated nor exotic – a few of the older rambler roses, beds of fuchsias, begonias and carnations. A complete, even refreshing, contrast to the lushness of the growth elsewhere in the garden.

Along the eastern side of the Walled Garden is a great *Cryptomeria japonica*. This, along with *Cunninghamia lanceolata* which is also represented here, were first discovered by James Cunningham, a ship's surgeon, as long ago as the early 1700s. Pressed specimens were placed in an herbarium, but not until 1826 were they thoroughly examined and Cunningham's find suitably acknowledged.

In this corner, too, is a Cabbage Palm (*Cordyline australis*), and elsewhere within the walls may be found a number of interesting plants and shrubs. Including the bulbous *Crinum* x *powellii*, with 45cm. stalks surmounted by whitish-pink trumpets up to 15cm. long; *Adenocarpus decorticans,* a Spanish member of the pea-family, with sprays of rich golden-yellow flowers and dense trifoliate leaves; two callistemons, the Bottle Brushes from Australia, *C. citrinus* with red flowers and a lemon scent from the crushed leaves, and *C. salignus,* one of the hardiest and most accommodating of the species, and sporting yellow flowers; and the half-hardy *Lobelia tupa*, with great scarlet flowers and grey downy leaves.

Leaving by the upper gate, past a wall clothed with the tiny, 8cm. carmine pink *Erinus alpinus,* from the western European mountains, one reaches a lawn – the Tennis Court Lawn. Here are other fine trees and shrubs, particularly *Desfontainia spinosa, Stranvaesia davidiana* and *Eucryphia* x *nymansensis* 'Nymansay'. In one corner is a conspicuous conifer with a distinctive bluish tinge, the Sitka Spruce (*Picea sitchensis*), in another the variegated form of *Griselinia littoralis,* a useful windbreak in many a west coast Scottish garden.

At the end of the Tennis Court Lawn is a small summer house. This is the best place from which to survey the Walled Garden at Brodick, and from here too can be seen tantalising glimpses of this lovely, rambling garden. Rightly the pride of Arran, and which came into the care of the National Trust for Scotland in 1958.

How to get there

British Rail ferry from ARDROSSAN to ISLE OF ARRAN. Thereafter 10 minute bus ride.

NINE

Branklyn *Perthshire*

A LITTLE over two kilometres from the centre of Perth, within sound, and nearly in sight, of the busy main road to Dundee, is what has been described as 'the finest two acres of private garden in the country'. This is Branklyn.

It was in 1922 that John and Dorothy Renton built and moved into Branklyn, an unpretentious modern house on the south slope of Kinnoull Hill overlooking the River Tay, a bare 60m. above sea level. Initially, the garden was very small, extending little beyond the end of the house itself, but over the years more ground was acquired. As Dorothy Renton described: 'There was no preconceived rule of design about the garden. It has been evolved gradually and the principal aim has been to give plants the proper conditions – it is primarily a home for plants.' But Dorothy Renton was too modest, Branklyn may have just 'growed', but it is quite clear that it grew under the hands of a master craftswoman; the balance and proportion of the existing garden is proof enough of that.

At the outset, as she went on to describe, 'The bishop weed and thistles grew the height of the gooseberry bushes and the whole flourished under a drapery of convolvulus', in the old orchard which they had taken over. Fortunately, beneath this undesirable groundcover, the soil was a good medium loam, quite acid, but on a fairly steep south to south-west slope overlying rock strata, which renders it liable to dry out quickly. Rainfall is on the average around 70 cm. (28in.) but in recent years has been nearer 50cm. (20in.), and frequent watering has proved necessary. On this promising, but awesome, foundation the Rentons set about creating what could be called a magnificent rock garden, but which is in reality a plantsman's paradise: a place of lovely vistas, of clever planting and of colour all the year round, of foliage contrast and subtle plant associations.

Dorothy Renton had long been a keen amateur botanist, but before coming to Branklyn had enjoyed little opportunity to garden in earnest, and none to display her remarkable talent for cultivating rare and difficult plants. This talent was fittingly acknowledged when she received the coveted Veitch Memorial Medal from the Royal Horticultural Society for her work in introducing and cultivating new plants; and the prestigious award by the Royal Caledonian Horticultural Society who made her one of the first recipients of the Scottish Horticultural Medal. John Renton, her husband, would deprecate his own part in the achievement of Branklyn, describing himself as a garden designer and calling his wife the real gardener of the family – but the result is one that could only have been achieved through a perfect horticultural partnership.

Dorothy Renton died in 1966, her husband in July the following year, but together they had made provision that Branklyn would be bequeathed to the National Trust for Scotland. Since that date the Trust has tended their garden with the same care and devotion that the Rentons gave over the forty-odd years of its creation. A number of improvements and ideas, which the Rentons had in mind but never carried out, have been incorporated, but the essential atmosphere of Branklyn has been most wonderfully preserved and only the most hardened visitor would be unimpressed by the flair, which was displayed by the Rentons in their choice of plants and plant associations. After a short while in the garden even the heavy hum of the traffic on the road below is forgotten in the fascination which is Branklyn.

Almost the first plant that a visitor sees after passing through the entrance gate is one to arouse his interest. This is a small bush, not unlike a miniature cupressus; on closer inspection, however, it turns out to be *Hebe cupressoides* – like most hebes a native of New Zealand, with long, slender, feathery branches and a profusion of pale blue flowers in June and July. Backed by *Rosa moyesii*, it is a telling combination. Behind is a *Cryptomeria japonica*. Further on, we come upon a specimen of the densely bushy *Pinus mugo (montana)*, the Mountain Pine from Central Europe, in the shade of which is another conifer, almost embracing a small rock, *Picea orientalis* 'Pendula', a slow-growing species with very close leaves and dense branches. Nearby is a *Eucryphia glutinosa,* providing shelter for hellebores, prostrate cotoneasters and the bracken-like fern *Polystichum aculeatum,* one of the good collection of ferns which are to be found in this garden – many of which are handsome enough to grace a suitably-sited mixed border. This is a field which is strangely neglected in most gardens.

The first of many fine maples, for which Branklyn is noted, is *Acer negundo* 'Auratum' (*A. californicum 'Aureum'*), a good yellow tree attaining forest size in the right situation. This is standing next to, that extraordinary conifer *Sciadopitys verticillata,* the Umbrella Pine. Conspicuous too in spring and early summer are three bushes of the golden philadelphus, *P. coronarius* 'Aureus', a lover, curiously, of dry soil and an excellent shrub in a dull corner.

A small water garden of great charm next greets the eye, bordered by Skunk Lily, *Lysichitum (Lysichiton) americanum,* beneath *Acer rubrum* – a most effective combination, enhanced here by an outstanding colony of *Lilium chalcedonicum* from Greece. This creates a memorable picture with its red turkscap flowers reflected in the dark water.

The path now diverges: one fork leads to the lower, the shadier and wetter portion of the garden, a place rich with hostas, colchicums, rodgersias and other plants; the other passes under a pergola which turns out to be support for a Cheal's Weeping Cherry (*Prunus* 'Kiku-shidare Sakura', to give it its real name) charming enough in its own right, but doubly so as the foot is smothered by *Cotoneaster horizontalis,* not the normal form, but the variant *C.h.* 'Variegata', a shrub which is far too little known, whose small green and white leaves suffuse with red in the autumn.

When Branklyn was started, so too was the great boom in rock gardens in this country. The time when exhibitors at Chelsea would show, and expect to sell, entire rock gardens, complete with plants, to wealthy clients. When the *doyen* of rock gardeners, Reginald Farrer, was thundering against the abominations that masqueraded as rock gardens and littered public park and private garden alike, calling the various types, with the utmost derision, the Dog's Grave or Devil's Lapful; the Drunkard's Dream – of 'noxious cement blocks', Plum Bun, or arrangements of Humpety-Dumpeties, or the Almond-Pudding 'Rockery' where ferns and Welsh poppies only will grow. Many are perpetuated or perpetrated today, but rarely derided with such delightful invective. The Rentons eschewed such fanciful monstrosities and proved themselves whole-hearted admirers and desciples of Farrer's more natural scree – but what a scree!

Built on the site where the Rentons had originally built a hard tennis-court, the rock garden itself was founded on rock which had come from a disused quarry several hundred metres above the house. Laboriously, with crow-bar and steam-engine, these massive boulders were inched down the hill and eased into their final positions. The screes themselves, on which Dorothy Renton grew so many of her fine plants, were constructed along the lines laid down by Farrer, and consisted of five parts of the rather sandy gravel from the nearby River Tay, added to one part of leaf soil and loam, the whole covered by more gravel. This, overlying a quick-drying soil on a gentle south-facing slope with good drainage, made Dorothy Renton's success possible. But nothing should be allowed to detract from her own great skill with difficult plants. Later, it is worth mentioning, she found that a richer soil mixture gave better results, so more soil and leaf mould was incorporated; but the gravel surface was retained to aid drainage.

Within the screes, have been created habitats for a great variety of plants: a true rock-gardeners' paradise, if ever there was one, with a wealth of fascinating, unusual and many very rare species. At the back is what must be one of the biggest specimens in the country of the dwarf weeping Eastern Hemlock, *Tsuga canadensis* 'Pendula', an enormous plant 5m. by 5m. But it is the small plants which will absorb enthusiast and plant-lover alike: *Oxalis adenophylla,* with delightful pink flowers over compact rosettes of crinkled grey leaves; the Pasque Flower, *Pulsatilla vulgaris,* in variety and in profusion; some of the collection of the dwarf rhododendrons, another Branklyn speciality, and which were one of Dorothy Renton's especial delights; the mat-forming *Geranium traversii elegans* from the Chatham Islands, with pink flowers 2cm. across and a grey-silvery leaf. To give contrast, here and there are fastigiate conifers, such as *Chamaecyparis pisifera* 'Aurea', and the soft-leaved *C.p.* 'Plumosa'. And, making its home in one corner, is one of the most beautiful plants of all and described by George Forrest who discovered it as 'the finest cliff plant of the whole range'. This is the quite staggeringly beautiful *Paraquilegia anemonoides,* whose deep blue flowers nodding on 7cm. stems over the richest green-grey foliage rosette are worth coming a very long way to see in spring. Normally a plant for the alpine house, here they thrive, increase and luxuriate. The source of these plants is from the subsequent introduction by Major Sheriff.

Other plants which usually cause comment are: *Hieracium waldsteinii,* an accommodating plant, given good drainage, with grey furry donkey-ear leaves and yellow dandelion flowers of 50cm. stems. There are also some 20 different species of celmisias in Branklyn, many of them in the screes, a magnificent genus, with many excellent and decorative members – all but a few natives of New Zealand and most with white daisy-like flowers. A plant from Central Asia of the thyme family which attracts a lot of attention is *Stellera chamaejasme,* a rhizomatous plant with stems 30 cm. high, with dense heads of pink buds which open to become charming white flowers.

Larger subjects in and around the screes, include a clump of *Camellia* × *williamsii* 'J. C. Williams', a single shell-pink camellia and a prolific flowerer in this garden. Nearby are two syringas, a huge *S. velutina (palibiniana)* some 1.8m. tall and nearly as much across, and *S.* × *persica,* the Persian Lilac. *Erica australis* 'Mr Robert', a beautiful white-flowered Tree Heath, is another eye-catcher. But throughout the planning the Rentons adhered to Farrer's precept that 'a dark hollow is doom and drip is damnation'.

By now it will be apparent that a visit to Branklyn is a unique and memorable experience. For fascinating plants abound in profusion: a spreading willow, *Salix lapponum* – the Lapland Willow, a rare native in this country; *Salix apoda,* a prostrate variety with glossy green leaves. This one has the delightful *Codonopsis convolvulacea forrestii* – growing through it, whose lavender-blue star-shaped 5cm. flowers are set off superbly (but how much more effective would it be growing through *Salix lanata*). Another codonopsis growing nearby is *C. tangshen,* another perennial twiner which can reach 3m., with greenish flowers with purple spots and stripes. Peonies are well represented, not only tree peonies, but also some of the less common species, including *P. veitchii* 'Woodwardii', the red *P. officinalis,* the white *P. emodi* from India. Many of these have interbred to create some excellent hybrids.

A little further on, and effectively dividing the garden, is a line of three pines, *Pinus rigida,* the Northern Pitch Pine from Eastern North America; *P. contorta,* the Beach Pine from Western America – a

Douglas introduction. and *P. peuce,* the Macedonian Pine from the Balkans. Together with *Genista aetnensis,* the Etna Broom, a 6m. specimen this, a successful break is created. This is enhanced by one of the most spectacular of Branklyn features – three mighty bushes of *Viburnum plicatum* 'Mariesii'. Botanically identical, they have slightly different flowering seasons, the lowest of all actually being good enough to start blooming in January, in a normal season.

And now we come to the start of the very comprehensive collection of dwarf and the smaller rhododendrons, for the cooler, drier conditions of the east of Scotland seem more to their liking than the lusher climate of the west. The larger-leaved species are not neglected and there are some fine plants of *RR. arizelum, fictolacteum, macabeanum* and the rose-coloured *R. rex.* But it is for the smaller species that Branklyn is most famous, and there are fine forms of *RR. campylogynum, primulaeflorum, racemosum* and *cephalanthum,* among a great many others, *R. griersonianum* is here too, as is the very beautiful *R. albrechtii.* But pride of place must go to a superb specimen of the lovely 'Temple Belle', an *orbiculatum × williamsianum* cross, with the leaf of the former and a darker pink flower than either parent; the bells have the consistency of the most exquisite porcelain.

Branklyn: the Upper Garden.

But it is as a garden for meconopsis that Branklyn has earned much of its reputation – not least for the beautiful blue strain of *M. grandis* 'Branklyn', which gained a First Class Certificate in 1963. The perennials in this family are represented by the 90cm. high yellow-flowered *M. chelidonifolia,* the shorter *M. villosa,* also yellow, the huge 120cm. and more *M. betonicifolia,* with vivid blue flowers, and its hybrids *M. × sarsonsii* and *M. × sheldonii,* as well as *M. quintuplinervia* with nodding blue single-headed flowers on 30cm. stems. The monocarpic species are seen at their best in May and June. These include the enormous *M. napaulensis,* fully 2m. tall and more, the 150cm. yellow *M. dhwojii, M. horridula* and *M. aculeata* – the last two seeding furiously, and, more often than not inconveniently, throughout the garden.

The upper levels are constructed as peat beds, and here is a treasure house of ericaceous plants: vacciniums, cassiopes including *C. fastigiata × wardii,* with square dark green stems with white heather flowers, a charming plant – the tongue-twisting *Omphalogramma vinciflorum,* with vivid violet flowers over primula-like rosettes of leaves, a native of the Himalayas; pernettyas, gaultherias and other peat-loving plants. And, of course, the primulas themselves, some common, some rare, but all delightful: *P. bhutanica,* a pale blue with a yellow eye; *P. edgworthii*; the Balkan, *P. frondosa; P. capitata,* and its close relative *P. sphaerocephala*; the highly desirable, but tricky, *P. vialii; PP. boothii, bracteosa, sonchifolia, nutans,* and more, many more. In one corner some jeffersonias can be found, the taller *J. diphylla,* some 15cm. high, which hails from Tennessee, and the shorter Manchurian, *J. dubia* and bare 7cm. high with flat 3cm. flowers of the clearest pale blue.

Some taller rhododendrons also grow here, including the charming, early-flowering 'Yellow Hammer', and a particularly fine form of the later-flowering yellow *R. campylocarpum.*

We now reach the end of the garden, where are some other rhododendrons and a number of taller trees, including one of the original apple trees, covered with a rampant *Hydrangea petiolaris,* fully 9m. tall and threatening to bring the whole lot crashing to the ground. Some interesting shrubs have been planted at this end of the garden, amongst others may be found: *Viburnum alnifolium,* the Hobble Bush, a moisture and half-shade lover, with huge velvety leaves, lacecap – hydrangea flowers and rich autumn colouring – a most desirable shrub, but not often seen; *Oxydendrum arboreum,*

11 *top* Crathes Castle. *Itea yunnanensis*, an unusual evergreen
 species growing in the yew border around the Fountain Garden
12 *above* Crathes Castle. A view of the Lower Garden with, in the
 foreground, the trunk of a fine *Eucalyptus gunnii*

13 Brodick Castle. *Rhododendron Lindleyi*

another beautiful and unusual shrub or small tree, with drooping white racemes of heather-like flowers in July and August; a *Euronymus phellomanus,* a Chinese shrub with cork-winged branches and great pink fruits; *Podocarpus alpinus, Trochodendron araliodes,* an excellent, architectural evergreen from Japan, with apple-green glossy foliage beloved of flower decorators; *Olearia virgata,* another most desirable member of this excellent family, at first glance resembling a tamarisk; two vacciniums, the dwarf *V. moupinense,* and the taller *V. ovatum,* yet another Douglas introduction from Western North America; and a very good, dark red *Kalmia latifolia,* as well as many others.

Among the 'herbaceous' plants in this part of the garden is the gigantic *Megacarpea polyandra,* fully 3m. tall, with panicles of greenish-yellow flowers. It is normally a shy flowerer, but at Branklyn seedlings are already beginning to appear. Another, as spectacular, if not so tall, is *Veratrum nigrum,* 2.5m high with rich purple-black, very evil-looking spikes over huge leaves. Its white relative *V. album* is also in the garden, and both yield poisons.

Other plants which will catch the eye are *Orchis maderensis,* a terrestrial orchid with spikes of purple flowers 25cm. long, and another, *Orchis elata,* similar in colour, but twice as tall. *Pyrola rotundifolia,* the round-leaved wintergreen, a rare and very fragrant native of these islands, is an intriguing little plant; *Asarum europaeum,* or snake root, is another of a sinister variety, with wicked purple-brown bells and a strong scent of resin.

The way leads back along the bottom of the garden. Here are further interesting plants including magnolias, *MM.* x *watsonii, sieboldii* and a great *sinensis,* which hangs over the path. Species and varieties of *Trillium, Colchicum, Sanguinaria, Iris* and *Helleborus* abound. Here too is the majority of Branklyn's fine collection of cyprepediums, including *CC. acaule, reginae, parviflora* and *pubescens.* A plant which will immediately strike the eye, at the lower end of the scree, is the delightful, and normally very delicate, *Corydalis cashmeriana,* with clear blue flowers over blue-green cut foliage – a very beautiful plant.

And so back to the house, where the stone troughs and borders furnish even more horticultural treasures. Here are some more *Paraquilegia anemonoides,* some plants of *Salix* x *boydii,* a small, gnarled and very slow-growing willow, found only once in the mountains of Angus in Scotland, not all that far from Branklyn; excellent plants of

Helichrysum milfordiae, Edraianthus serpyllifolia, a member of the campanula family, a dwarf, mat-forming plant with rich purple flowers, a most desirable resident of the Balkans; *Rhodothamnus chamaecistus; Thalictrum kiusianum; Drapetes dieffenbachii; Phyteuma comosum,* from Dalmatia; *Calceolaria darwinii; Gentiana saxosa,* a white-flowered New Zealand species; *Soldanella montana; Draba sundermanii* and *Daphne arbuscula,* to mention just a few. A list which will make any alpine enthusiast's mouth water.

More mundane, but none the less effective, is the planting of the narrow border by the house. Here can be found the grey-leaved *Olearia mollis* and the striking 90cm. tall *Hebe glaucophylla* 'Variegata'. A grouping of the rose 'Nypels Perfection' is remarkably effective against the house all covered with *Cytisus battandieri* and the grey-leaved *Lonicera splendida,* (which is, unfortunately, not as hardy as one would like).

From here it is only a few metres to the upper grass path and a sundial. On the way one will pass a magnificent, 5m.-high *Hydrangea sargentiana,* which never fails to produce a wonderful display of flowers. Behind is an excellent colouring, and flowering, bush of *Pieris formosa forrestii. Corokia cotoneaster, Clethra delavayi,* and two unusual grey-leaved shrubs, *Olearia moschata* and *Senecio monroi,* both New Zealanders, are planted together overlooking the scree. Nearby is a magnificent specimen of that highly desirable rhododendron, *R. williamsianum,* one of the Thomsonii series with quite beautiful shell-pink hanging bells. This is planted next door to *Primula* x 'Garryarde Guinevere' – a most effective combination. Most significant of all along this path are great mounds of *Acer palmatum* 'Dissectum'. These must date from very near the inception of the Rentons' garden.

But to me, the most striking thing about Branklyn is that it remains a personal garden – despite belonging to a national body. This is almost wholly due to the Trust's representative, Stewart Annand, who through his knowledge, and by his enthusiasm and devotion, care and hard work, has made the garden his own. By developing and extending the network of gardening friends which the Rentons had started, the range of plants at Branklyn has been greatly enlarged. Here, growing to perfection, and evidently completely happy in their new surroundings, are treasures from New Zealand, from the High Andes, from the Himalayas and from many other parts of the world. This interchange of plant traffic, of information and material – the freemasonry of gardening – is now on a considerable scale. The Rentons would have been proud to see their legacy today.

How to get there

In city of PERTH, off Dundee Road *(A85)*

TEN

Tyninghame *East Lothian*

FORTY-SEVEN kilometres east of Edinburgh, on the shores of the Firth of Forth near a bay of the sea named Hedderwick Bay, and a short distance north of the ancient town of Dunbar, lies Tyninghame, home of the Earls of Haddington for nearly 350 years and the setting for one of the most exciting gardens in Scotland. This coast of East Lothian is steeped in ancient history. Vikings, Danes and Normans, in their time, have landed, ravished and departed. The early Christian settlements, of which Tyninghame was one, were more often than not the target. In the year 941 it was the turn of the Danes, who razed the village of Tyninghame, then situated between the present house and the bay, and destroyed the church founded three centuries earlier by St Baldred of the Bass, an early Christian teacher who has given his name to many a feature around. In later years, another religious order settled – the Monks of Tyninghame – and the remains of a Norman Church stands to this day below the house. Beneath the two arches of the old church – the dog-tooth carving still wonderfully preserved – is the site of the family burial ground. This is a place apart, a place with an atmosphere of great tranquillity and sanctity.

Guarded by a magnificent ilex of a venerable age, this holy site is approached by an avenue of lime trees; but instead of the standard trees, which normally comprise an avenue, being allowed to rest alone, alternate ones have been kept at bush height and in bush form. The effect is original and remarkably effective – such imaginative touches combined with high taste are a characteristic of Tyninghame.

In 1628, Thomas, first Earl of Haddington, then Earl of Melrose and an intimate of King James VI of Scotland (James I of England) purchased the property, and since that date it has been the principal residence of the Earls of Haddington. The imposing house, on a rise of ground north of the Tyne salt flats, is of mellow red stone, with distinctive turrets and typical crow-stepped gables. It was believed to have once been a monastery; when the monks departed it became a dwelling house. In 1829 it was placed in the hands of William Burn, the distinguished Scottish architect, and it was he who created the house as it stands today. It was at one time thought that the alterations he carried out had been extensive, but recently the original drawings have been discovered and it was found out that all he in effect did was to add the two bay windows on the western side; that the corner turrets so long believed to have been his work had in fact belonged to an earlier period.

For centuries, forestry has been a close concern of the Earls of Haddington. Most of the magnificent trees in the area around the house and elsewhere on the estate were planted by the 6th Earl in 1707, the year of the Union with England, and it is clear that he was one of the great pioneer foresters in Scotland. A book he wrote on forest trees in 1732* is crammed with sound and still relevant advice and ideas. It is probable that his views had widespread influence, particularly in popularising the Scots Fir – although his early method of drying the seed indoors, in front of an open fire, was hazardous in the extreme, and nearly burnt his house down.

It was the 6th Earl who planted the Long Avenue, to the north of the house. It is 2.5 km. in length, and at one end stands an obelisk to his memory, while the other, on a hot day, fades into the shimmering distance, a vista of beeches and blue – the blue of the sea and the sky. As the walker nears the seaward end, he will become aware of another colour too: a thin line of pink which broadens until it is revealed as a drift of the common thrift (*Armeria maritima*) growing on the saltings for almost a kilometre at low tide. From here it is a short walk to Whitberry Point where the full sweep of the East Lothian coast can be seen. To the north lies Tantallon Castle, a renowned name in Scottish history, and the Bass Rock, a black, brooding place with an almost mesmeric effect even on the brightest of sunlit days. Below lies a stack of rocks, St Baldred's Cradle,

* *Some Directions about Raising Forest Trees* by Thomas Hamilton, 6th Earl of Haddington. Recently reprinted, and edited by Professor M. L. Anderson (Thomas Nelson, 1953).

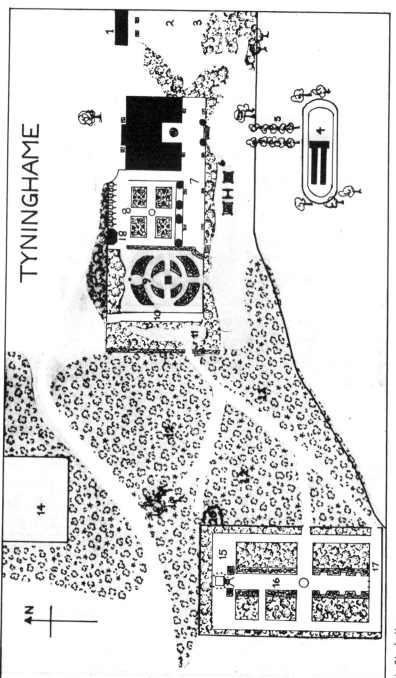

TYNINGHAME

N

1. Clock House
2. East Shrub Border
3. Heather Bed
5. Lime Avenue
6. Long Border
7. Bay Walk
9. Lady Haddingtons Garden
10. Apple Arbour
11. White Garden
13. Laburnum Avenue
14. Bowling Green
15. Walled Garden
17. Apple Walk
18. Summer House
19. New Shrub and Tree

innocuous in calm weather, but a seething cauldron of turbulent water in a gale.

From here, too, can be seen the extensive woods which the 6th Earl planted to the north and east of the present house. Despite the desire for timber during the last war, and the ravages of devastating gales in 1968 and 1973, much of it is still standing and provides the essential shelter for the garden. East Lothian, by repute the 'Garden of Scotland', whose rich and fertile soil has long provided produce for Edinburgh and further afield, boasts a light, sandy loam. There is a general lack of humus and natural fertility in the Tyninghame garden, this, combined with a very low rainfall – 60cm. (24in.) a year – and quick drainage, poses its problems. Loads of peat, manure, compost and spent hops are essential additions in providing the necessary moisture. But the climate is generally temperate and there is little snow. Frosts are no bother; although late spring frosts do occur, they are seldom severe due to the protection around the house and the presence of the sea. Fortunately, too, the garden is far enough from the shore for salt-spray not to prove a factor. But there is one peril the gardener has in full measure – the bitingly cold north and east winds, often of gale force, which in spring are the bane of this part of Scotland. This is a killing wind. Young and precocious shoots can be snapped back, buds browned and a trail of irreparable damage caused in a single night. A devastation only exceeded by the periodic invasions of deer, rabbits, hares, pigeons and the other denizens of Tyninghame.

When the present Earl came to live at Tyninghame in 1952, to the east of the house lay a confusion of laurel – a relic of Victorian planting – which in places had encroached nearly to the lower windows. In the midst of this tangle could be seen one or two fine beech, oak, Spanish chestnuts and sycamores, as well as some smaller *Arbutus unedo*, of uncertain age. The tangle was cleared, a vista created and great curving shrub beds designed; then trees were planted – principally acers and sorbus, including *S. sargentiana* and *S.* 'Joseph Rock', and *Acer rubrum* and *A. grosseri*, a particularly beautiful, 'Snake Bark'. This is now primarily a part of the garden for autumn colour, and magnificent it looks in season. On the northern side, beyond what had once been a rockery before it was levelled, and well-protected from the east, stand three fine specimens of the large-leaved *Rhododendron macabeanum*. Now twelve years old, in 1974 they produced their trusses of magnificent yellow bell flowers for the first time.

Particularly effective is a long, narrow bed of heather planted among a number of *Pinus pinea,* the Stone Pine from the Mediterranean shores, the seeds of these were brought from Florence fifteen years ago.

The clearing of this vista has exposed the very attractive Clock House. One time the laundry to Tyninghame, it has now been restored to make a dower house of immense charm, with a formal paving and Versailles tubs filled with bay trees, which survive outdoors the rigours of winter with apparent content. Between the Clock House and the side of the east wing lies a large, triangular border which gives a foretaste of the prevailing planting theme at Tyninghame – a theme which eschews harsh and bright colours and favours the softer tones of blues, greys, pinks and whites, with, in their place, the quieter yellows. In this instance, the effect is from *Buddleia* 'Lochinch', rosemary, santolina and cat-mint, as well as roses including the Floribunda 'Elizabeth of Glamis' and an old Hybrid Tea 'Wellworth' – a magnificent cream-coloured rose quite happy grown as a shrub.

A path runs from the east side of the house through two shrub borders, past some silver-grey leaved celmisias and a huge rose 'Fruhlingsgold', to a sheltered, south-facing nook. This is home to some fine clumps of *Myosotidium hortensia (nobile)* – the Chatham Island Forget-me-not. A present from Inverewe, it clearly delights in the climate and sandy soil of Tyninghame and is given pride of place among a collection of shrubs: ceanothus, cistus, buddleia, with a backdrop of *Vitis vinifera* 'Purpurea' and nearby some *Lilium* × *testaceum* and the rose 'Chinatown' – a good combination,.

We now come to the Long Border. Although the overall effect in high summer is of a drift of colour, the detailed grouping bears very close examination. Outside the border itself, on the grass of the lower terrace, are two ancient, raised stone beds. A picture of the garden at the turn of the century shows these full of bedding plants; the planting scheme now is more subtle, and more effective. Each bed is filled with the green and grey leaves of lavender and santolina, each corner is graced with huge specimens of *Cotinus coggygria* 'Notcutt's Variety'. A further bed between the two, in the shape of the letter 'H' is planted with the same cotinus. This planting provides contrast and balance to the glory of the Long Border behind.

The serpentine edge of this border creates a varying depth, this is accentuated by the clever placing of four horseshoe-shaped metal arches. These, smothered with roses, clematis, honeysuckle and, sometimes, *Vitis coignetiae,* have the effect of breaking the considerable length into 'bays'. Within each 'bay', and between them, are mixed plantings of shrub roses, lilies, delphiniums, *Romneya coulteri* – which thrives here – and agapanthus, both *A. campanulatus* and *A. orientalis,* which also do well. One 'bay' may have a planting of grey-leaved sub-shrubs; senecios, artemisias, verbascums and helichrysums, with lilies growing through them; another will be planted with roses, 'Aloha', 'Chinatown', 'The New Dawn', 'Lady Hillingdon' or the deep pink 'Parade'. The Long Border at Tyninghame is a wonderful sight in summer.

Steps at the end lead up to the Bay Walk. Seated on one of the benches at either end, one can appreciate how clever has been the design here. No ordered riot of colour, as in the Long Border below, instead, an austere and stark path of red gravel, on which are placed bay trees in Versailles tubs. A thin border of grass separates these from lavender (*Lavandula spica* 'Hidcote') and a hedge of shrub roses, the Floribundas 'Chinatown' and 'Iceberg', the Hybrid Musk 'Felicia', interspersed on the upper side with standard *Pyrus salicifolia* 'Pendula'. The prevailing colours are thus yellow and white, grey and light blue; the result is soft. The architectural impact of the path with its ultra-formal planting creates a striking contrast with the heavy ornamentation of the house. It is a simple design, but perfect in this setting.

Down this path, and opposite another flight of steps, which leads to the lower terrace and the Long Border through two sentinel Irish yews, lies a cobbled courtyard between the southern wings of the house. Protected from draught by a huge *Garrya elliptica,* in the warmth and shade grow a number of interesting shrubs: *Senecio hectorii*; *Jasminium* × *stephanense,* a pink climber; *Lonicera japonica halliana* and *Hydrangea villosa.* At the foot of a fine Venetian well-head scrambles *Ceanothus prostratus.*

Retracing one's steps and ascending another level, one finds oneself on the upper terrace, or Parterre. Dominating all, stands a tall and curious sundial, copied in 1800 from the famous one at Newbattle Abbey. Around this centrepiece are parterre beds, planted with a white and yellow colour scheme of roses surrounded by a low hedge of the Golden Box. The roses are the ubiquitous, but none the less superb, Floribunda 'Iceberg' and the Hybrid Tea 'King's Ransom', with the beautiful 'Leverkusen' – a Kordes introduction of 1954 whose dark shiny leaves are a perfect foil to the lighter foliage of 'Iceberg'. Here, 'Leverkusen' is grown on stout supports to give added height. On the west wall of the house are more interesting shrubs and roses: *Osmanthus delavayi, Escallonia* 'Apple Blossom', and *Rosmarinus lavandulaceus,* the prostrate rosemary, growing out over the paving.

In the far corner lies a Summer House behind which grows and flowers luxuriantly the red 'Lobster Claw' of *Clianthus puniceus*. That this will thrive, and flower, here gives some idea of how generally soft is the climate in this part of Scotland.

A small gate leads from the Summer House to Lady Haddington's Garden. For years this had been a piece of nondescript, rough ground, inviting inspiration. So, being a lover of old-fashioned roses, Lady Haddington decided that here she must create her own rose garden. But like so many intentions in gardening, the obstacles rapidly became more formidable than had at first been realised for: very soon they came across the foundations of an old grass tennis court, which had to be painfully extracted, stone by stone. The general design of the new garden was taken from an old French gardening book found in the library at Tyninghame. The wooden arbour in the centre was built by the estate carpenter. It shades a white marble statue representing Summer which was brought from Vicenza in Italy. The beds maintain the original design, but, by planting with tall shrub roses, and creating a number of arches, the effect is of being in Arcady, a glorious, heavily-scented maze in a country far-removed from Scotland.

Once again, the prevailing Tyninghame colours have been used. Individual planting associations abound. Here is a mixed planting of lavenders, their differing leaves providing subtleties of colour and texture. Tree peonies vie with deutzias, clamatis and honeysuckles climb pillars and arches, lilies grow through pinks and grey-leaved plants. For the most part, the roses are old-fashioned, but to continue the flowering season a number of modern shrub roses have been included. On the top side is a basin of running water, which runs through a stone bowl shaped like a primitive head. In another strategic position, a large vase overflows with a profusion of pelargonium, cherry pie and *Helichrysum petiolatum*. To visit this garden in high summer, and it is at its best in July and August, is a truly memorable experience.

Leading from it, away from the house, is an arbour of pleached apple trees. Joining now at the top, they too provide shade and contrast with the glories of the neighbouring rose garden. But this arbour, too, has its subtleties, and is under-planted with honeysuckles and roses.

Clearly, in such a garden and with such a talented garden creator, there must be a place where white predominates and, sure enough, and in the most perfect setting, there is a white corner. This is of the white lilac, *Syringa vulgaris* 'Monique Lemoine', *Buddleia* 'Lochinch', to provide a light-grey foliage, white phlox and white delphiniums. The lavender-blue flowers of *Hebe hulkeana* provide a foil and contrast with the prevailing white, and the parallel branches of *Viburnum plicatum* 'Mariesii' provide contrast of another form. Conspicuous too, in this part of the garden, is a large stand of *Lilium* 'Mrs R. O. Backhouse'. Another corner has an equally effective association of white lilac, white meconopsis, mixed grey-leaved sub-shrubs and the grey-blue foliage of *Paeonia mlokosewitschii*.

A gate at the further side leads to the Wilderness, which was originally laid out by Lady Haddington, wife of the 6th Earl, at the same time as the main planting of the woods, in 1707. The Wilderness plantation was a characteristic method of planting at this period. In his book, which has been previously referred to, Lord Haddington gives credit for the introduction of the Wilderness to the Earl of Mar who was a keen tree planter on his Alloa estates. 'They have not been long introduced into this Country', he goes on to say (1732), 'and the Way they were at first laid out was, there was a Center, Straight Walks from it, Ending on as good Views as could be had. There were also Serpentine Walks that run through the whole Hedged, as the Straight Walks were, and the Angles with Trees of Different Shades mixt. Now I hear they are Weary of the Hedges, but as Every one doth what he thinks best, People are at Liberty, but the People who make it their Business to lay out Ground for Gentlemen, are in my Opinion very unfit for it. They are too formal, and Stiff, besides they make Every thing so Busy, that they croud the ground too much' – a point of profound home-spun wisdom as relevant today as it was then.

The Wilderness at Tyninghame first consisted of a centre near the existing Bowling Green with fourteen walks coming from it, although whether these were straight or 'serpentine' is not revealed. The Bowling Green was formerly surrounded by a high yew hedge, this has been removed and only the corner yews remain. Surrounding it are many magnificent trees, some still with the rocks which were originally placed to anchor them in their infancy against the devastating East Lothian gales. In spring, the close-cropped springy turf is carpeted with a profusion of coloured primroses, a renowned strain in Victorian times when they were the primrose proper, with no trace of the polyanthus among them.

In spring too, elsewhere, the wild flowers are permitted to grow. The approach down the main drive with the cherries in full flower, the red gravel of the surface and a white and blue carpet – the blue of that pernicious weed, in other spots, the creeping speedwell, the white from the common daisy – is a wonderful sight, a bonus to the better-known delights of Tyninghame. And in another part of the park flourishes the wild tulip, *Tulipa sylvestris,* it too used to carpet the Wilderness.

No underplanting had hitherto been made under the canopy of the great trees in the Wilderness, but over recent years this has been remedied. Now, beneath the shade of the 6th Earl's legacy, lie a wealth of bulbs, herbaceous plants, shrubs and roses. One path is lined with azaleas. In another spot camellias flourish – principally the *C.* × *williamsii* cultivars. Meconopsis and tree peonies, hostas and bergenias rub shoulders with hydrangeas, *H. villosa,* and the variegated leaved 'Maculata', a most effective shrub for long range planting. Huge stands of roses; the Rugosa 'Blanc Double de Coubert' and the pink scented modern shrub rose 'Erfurt'; 'Complicata', which is believed to be a *R. macrantha* or, perhaps, *R. canina* hybrid, whose single 13cm. wide pink flowers are very striking, this is an admirable old rose. Among the better-known are 'Nevada', 'Fruhlingsgold', a colossal and invasive *R. filipes* 'Kiftsgate', and many others. Here too is a fine *Parrotia persica* and several sorbus, including *S. sargentiana,* whose scarlet berries and rich red colouring is sensational later in the year, as well as acers, weigelas and philadelphus in profusion.

Bearing right-handed, is a recent planting of *Viburnum plicatum* 'Mariesii', with sorbus behind, the whole dominated by large weeping elm, *Ulmus glabra* 'Camperdownii'. This leads to a young avenue of laburnums, which in ten or so years' time will be yet another feature to add to the many Tyninghame enjoys – that is, if the remarkably athletic Tyninghame rabbits leave them alone, for it is worth mentioning in passing, that the 6th Earl would plant laburnums among his other, more precious trees as he found that rabbits preferred them to all others.

Tyninghame: the greenhouse at the end of the Yew Allée.

And so to the Walled Garden. Dating from 1660, this is one of Tyninghame's principal attractions. Passing through a new planting of sorbus with an underplanting of mixed hypericums, one enters the huge, two hectare, old brick-walled garden. Running to the bottom is an immense yew allée, clipped smooth except where niches are being grown to hide some white marble statues. In the centre is a marble fountain. This length use to hold two stupendous herbaceous borders which, in their day, were a wonderful sight. But wartime economies sounded their death knell and now the centre is grassed down, creating a powerful, formal effect.

At the top end is a greenhouse surrounded by ten remarkably even Italian Cypresses (*Cupressus sempervirens*), some 9m. high and over 100 years old. Bound tightly with wire, and clipped once a year, they provide the perfect focal point to the long yew walk. But they are dwarfed by an enormous *Cercidiphyllum japonicum*. Proceeding towards the yew walk one passes some formal box-bound enclosures occupied by standard mulberries – an interesting combination – the main feature of which was brought from Belgium. On the right, where an old vinery stood, is the embryo beginning of a border for tender shrubs, *Buddleia crispa* and *B. auriculata,* and the Loquat, *Eriobotrya japonica.* To the left the site of an old melon house, a centre border has been planted with old-fashioned and other roses, 'Aloha', 'Coral Dawn' and others, which will arch over and meet a line of *Buddleia* 'Lochinch', thus creating an ingenious arcade of colour and scent.

To the left of the centre fountain, which is of eighteenth-century Florentine origin, is a grassy path leading to an iron gate. On either side are narrow borders. Once again the predominant theme is pink and grey and white. This from globe artichokes, pink lavender, and roses: 'The New Dawn' and the Dwarf Polyantha 'The Fairy', which grows a bare 46 cm., and is an ideal edger. At the back, to give added distinction, are more *Pyrus salicifolia* 'Pendula'.

Beyond the marble fountain, along the entire length of the garden, and in an area once devoted to raspberries, is a new planting. The design was laid out by the eminent landscape gardener James Russell, and the huge, irregular, curved beds hold a treasury of plants. Chief among them is a magnificent collection of the newer cultivars of bearded iris from Italy, which are most telling *en masse.* And there are many interesting and unusual trees and shrubs enjoying what must be one of the most sheltered positions at Tyninghame. Among them may be found: *Drimys winteri; Acer hersii, A. nikoense* (the Nikko Maple), *A. palmatum* 'Heptalobum Osakazuki' and others. *Stuartia pseudocamellia, Cornus spp.,* virburnums, corylopsis, both *C. pauciflora* and *C. wilmottiae.* There are also two 'Fossil' trees; the remarkable Maidenhair Tree, *Ginkgo biloba* and the Dawn Redwood, *Metasequoia gyptostroboides,* which was discovered as recently as 1941 in the depths of China. Planted at first as something of an exciting oddity, the full value of the tree for garden decoration is now firmly established. Of a delicious light green colour at the beginning of the summer, it colours magnificently in the autumn to old gold through various intermediate stages of tawny pink.

In these beds, too, is the bulk of Lord Haddington's collection of Eucalpytus, to which he has devoted a great deal of attention. Fully at home, as might be expected, are *EE. gunnii, parviflora, pauciflora* and *subcrenulata*. Less likely, but still doing well at Tyninghame are *E. perriniana* and *E. coccifera*.

At the bottom of the Yew Allée is an iron gate leading from the walled garden to what is probably the chief and best known of Tyninghame features: the Apple Walk. Over 90m. long, close planted with espalier apple trees, this tunnel is a remarkable sight at any time of the year; especially at blossom time and at petal fall when the whole walk is a carpet of pink. In summer, when the fruit is swelling and when the dappled shade hides the two white marble statues of Flora and Ganymede at either end, an atmosphere of almost monastic peace and coolness and calm descends.

Out of the Apple Walk, past a fine Aralia and a rose hedge of *Rosa foliolosa,* an unusual and effective ground-cover for a shady spot, back again to the Wilderness. The end too of a memorable garden tour, where every grouping, every corner and border reveals a gardening and design talent, a feel for tone and balance, for texture and plant association of a very high order.

The similarity to the treatment of the Crathes' borders is striking. Here is a similar skill in planting, planning and plant knowledge. But Tyninghame lacks the tight, formal setting which the Burnett Leys inherited. There is much more movement in the Tyninghame garden, flowing lines, vistas and space to play with, this is a modern idiom, but through it all one sees the hand of a very knowledgeable plant-lover.

How to get there

10 km west of DUNBAR; 42 km east of EDINBURGH
Turn off *A1* (HADDINGTON-DUNBAR) 11 km east of HADDINGTON

14 Brodick Castle. The Water Garden

15 *top* Tyninghame. A view in Lady Haddington's Garden
16 *above* Tyninghame. The famous Apple Walk

17 *top* Branklyn. A general view of the Scree

18 *above* Branklyn. *Meconopsis x sheldonii*

19 *top* Doune. Looking towards the Arboretum

20 *above* Doune. The Glen of the Buchany Burn in Spring

ELEVEN

Doune *Perthshire*

A PRINCIPAL attraction on the Scottish leisure scene is the Motor Museum at Doune in Perthshire, home of the Earl of Moray. Annually the Museum itself, the Hill Climbs and kindred activities draw huge crowds, but over the last few years an increasing number of visitors have also come to see the neighbouring Doune Park Gardens which are rapidly, and rightly, assuming a growing reputation in Scottish gardening.

The Morays are one of the oldest and most distinguished of the great Scottish families, twice descended from the Stewarts, the Royal House of Scotland. The first mention of their castle at Doune is in 1381, and it was clearly a fortress of great political and economic importance, for in the Middle Ages Doune, in the valley of the River Teith (a tributary of the great Forth) guarded the two main routes into the Highlands; that from Edinburgh to Inverlochy Castle near the present Fort William, and that from Glasgow by way of Perth to Inverness. The castle was built by Robert Stewart, the most powerful figure in the Scotland of his day and uncle, some say murderer, of that same Duke of Rothesay who died under such mysterious circumstances at Falkland Palace, 60 kilometres to the east in Fife.

Doune Castle figures frequently in the history of Scotland during the fifteenth and sixteenth centuries; as a state prison, or as a dower house, and it was a favourite stopping place for King James II when he came to hunt deer in the forests around Doune and Stirling. There is a brief mention in the castle records of a garden where leeks, cabbages – more probably, the ubiquitous kail – and onions were grown. Wages were paid to a gardener, a park-keeper and, of course, to a jailor in those days. Mary Queen of Scots certainly stayed at Doune on several occasions, and the suite of rooms above the kitchen today is still known as Queen Mary's Apartments. In 1592, the Stewart of the day was created 1st Earl of Moray, and it is the 20th Earl of Moray who now possesses the Castle and the estates of Doune.

In Bonnie Prince Charlie's uprising of 1745, the Jacobites seized Doune Castle and used it as a prison. At a later date, the great Scottish writer, Sir Walter Scott, worked it into his novel *Waverley*, and immortalised the area in his well-known poem *The Lady of the Lake*. Repairs on the castle were carried out from time to time during the first half of the eighteenth century, but evidently to no avail and gradually the old fortress fell into disuse and disrepair; it was not restored to its present condition until 1883, by the Edinburgh architect Andrew Kerr. So ruinous now was the castle that it could no longer be lived in, so it came about that the 10th Earl of Moray decided in 1802 to build on the site of the present Doune House, some five kilometres west of Doune Castle and the little town of Doune.

The policies at first consisted of a Walled Garden, and little else. Then the meadows on either side of the delightfully named Buchany Burn were levelled and drained. Then, rather more than a century ago, a pinetum was started: over the years an impressive collection of conifers have thrived and some are of a huge size.

The 17th Earl, himself a botanist, commenced the planting of the glen in 1920. By the late 1920s this was nearly completed and the Japanese Garden at the top of the glen developing nicely, but his death in 1931 put a stop to everything. From then on, and through the war years, the garden at Doune became increasingly neglected, the once-fine planting overgrown, and the walled-garden itself ploughed up and used as a nursery for the commercial woodlands of Doune estate. It was in 1968 that the major task of restoring the Doune Park Gardens was begun. Under the talented leadership of the Gardens Manager, Bill Edgar, who is well known in Scottish gardening circles as writer, lecturer and broadcaster on gardening subjects, the garden at Doune has gone from strength to strength.

Doune lies on the northern bank of the River Teith where (to quote from *The Lady of the Lake*)

> *Mountains that like giants stand*
> *to sentinel enchanted lands*

These are the Ochills, the Trossachs and the Fintry Hills, whose highest peaks sound like poetry itself: Ben Cleuch, Creag Beinn nan Eun, Ben Vorlich, Meall Odhar, Beinn Each, Ben Ledi . . . 'rising ridge on ridge', and the highest of them all at 961m., Beinn Dearg, Stronend, and Cringate Law. This protection on three sides means that Doune is little troubled by snow. The gardens, though, are in a hollow – a true frost pocket – and it is a late garden, some three weeks behind others in the Forth Valley. The Walled Garden itself provides good protection, but, as so often happens, within the walls the plants require firm staking to cope with gusts of wind which swirl around from all directions. Wind otherwise is of little bother, except on the higher ground where the great gales of 1968 and 1973 wrought havoc here as elsewhere in Scotland; but for the most part the wind blows harmlessly over the garden and the glen of the Buchany Burn. But in spring, the north-easterly blow is a killer. The soil is slightly acid, tending on the light side with sand and gravel predominating. The sub-soil is an easy one to work with, and in a normal year an average of rather more than one metre of rain can be relied on in these foothills of the Trossachs.

The siting of the garden some 900m. from the modern complex of the Motor Museum, poses a number of problems of considerable commercial importance, the most pressing being how to attract people over the intervening distance. For, although many now come to see the gardens themselves, others are primarily interested in the Motor Museum.

In 1968, when it was decided to turn the gardens into a commercial undertaking, the Walled Garden was obscured from the general view by a few trees, a scruffy hedge and wilderness. The first task was therefore to clear the stumps and scrub. At the same time, the top soil from round about, to the depth of 30cm. or so and consisting largely of nettles, briars and docks, was scraped into a convenient hollow. Thus a vista was created. A few of the better trees, a couple of Douglas Fir and a lime were preserved, the rest of the area put down to a wide sweep of lawn. A white-painted fence was built, Highland cattle were imported to give an extra interest, an Alder Walk added to draw, to entice people towards the Walled Garden and the Glen beyond. Drifts of daffodils were planted to enhance the effect in spring, and great splashes of dominant colours used in the planting scheme outside the Walled Garden.

This last effect was achieved from large, powerful groupings of

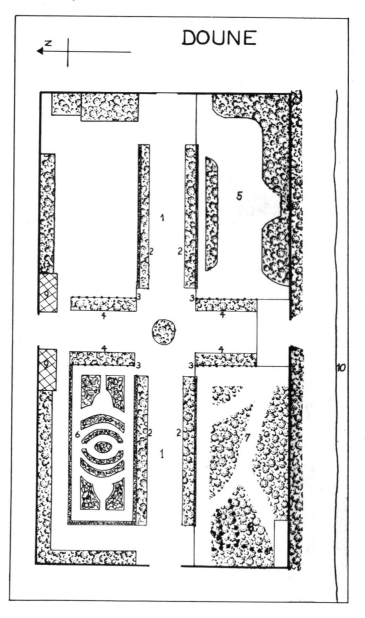

DOUNE

1. Gravel Walks
2. Herbaceous Borders
3. Rose Pergola
4. Annual Borders
5. Autumn Garden
6. Rose Garden
7. Shrub Garden
8. Stepping Stone Bed
9. Greenhouses
10. Buchany Burn

shrubs; from *Olearia* x *haastii; Hypericum* 'Hidcote'; *Berberis darwinii;* the pink-budded, white flowered *Escallonia* 'Donald Seedling'; and two cotoneasters, *C. salicifolius flocossus* with a somewhat ethereal effect from its wand-like branches and the denser, dark-green-leaved *C. wardii,* with bright orange-red berries. At the back, among other climbers, are two roses, 'Parkdirektor Riggers', a deep, deep red, and 'Ritter von Barmstede' an almost perpetually flowering pink. The overall effect of this massed planting is of an irrestistible splash of colour, which can be seen from as far away as the Motor Museum.

Within the walls, the traditional Walled Garden with flowers, fruit and vegetables have been preserved, but the latter are reserved for only one of the four segments of the area which is one hectare in extent.

The remainder is devoted to a Rose Garden, a Shrub Garden and an Autumn Garden. Down the centre runs a double and quite wide herbaceous border of perennials, and peonies and a number of white shrub roses, interspersed with annuals – the whole chosen to create a balanced and mixed colour scheme and backed by a hedge of the blue-grey *Chamaecyparis lawsoniana* 'Allumii'. This leads to the Rose Pergola running north-south across the width of the walled-garden. On each corner is the apple-scented rambler 'Francis E. Lester' with great clusters of single pinkish-white flowers. The intention here has been to have the hotter colours at the top: so one side commences with the reds and descends through pink to white, while the other starts with rich golds and yellows, fading again to white. The effect is most satisfying. Only the tried and true ramblers and climbers have been used on this pergola; those such as 'The New Dawn', 'Albertine', 'Alberic Barbier', and some of the more modern, including several Shrub Roses, 'Leverkusen', the brilliant orange-red 'Danse du Feu', 'Dortmund', a single red with a white eye, 'Joseph's Coat' and 'Maigold' which has the distinctive spinossima scent. All of these have proved reliable, furnish well and do not become leggy.

The Rose Garden within its surround of the Pergola and a hedge of *x Cupressocyparis leylandii* is designed in concentric box-edged beds. In the centre is the brilliant red Floribunda 'Korona'; the outer beds are devoted to yellow and white roses: 'Iceberg', 'Pascali', 'Virgo' 'Royal Highness' as whites, 'Allgold' 'Grandpa Dickson', 'Summer Sunshine', Sutter's Gold' and 'King's Ransom' doing duty for yellow. The solid beds at either end contain the hot-coloured 'Mr Lincoln', 'Ena Harkness', and the brilliant turkey-red, beautifully-scented almost perpetually flowering 'Ernest H. Morse'. On the corners are Floribundas, lightened with Shrub Roses – particularly the *R. alba,* 'Celestial', the Rugosa 'Blanc Double de Coubert' (a great favourite this), more 'Iceberg' and *Rosa alba* 'Maxima' – the Great Double White or "Jacobite" Rose which was supposed to feature in the garden of every true follower of 'The King over the Water'. These create a screen, so that the only way to see the Rose Garden is actually to enter it. Throughout, there is close planting and – a touch of effective originality – the heights are varied so that the lowest rose is by no means necessarily at the front of the bed, the tallest at the rear. This gives added interest to the planting and adds a spirit of exploration to the Rose Garden at Doune. Edging the roses are a number of grey-leaved plants, geraniums, *Nepeta nervosa, Verbena villosa* and other shrubby and herbaceous subjects.

A rule in Doune garden, and one that should be more widely copied, is that on every corner and at every entry to another part of the garden, there should be something sensational, a feature plant, certainly in appearance and, if possible, in fragrance. Thus behind the Rose Garden and in the wide borders in that corner of the garden we first find a large group of the deliciously fragrant *Philadelphus coronarius,* whose quite small creamy-white flowers come out a good two to three weeks earlier than the better-known hybrids 'Belle Etoile' and 'Virginal', both of which are represented elsewhere.

These are borders crammed full of clever plant associations: the 90cm. *Hebe ochracea,* with bright golden-green closely over-lapping tiny leaves (not unlike those of a cassiope) and white flowers, is planted against *Berberis thunbergii atropurpurea:* Rose 'Nevada' grows behind *Senecio laxifolius* in a corner, with the silver-leaved *Cytisus battandieri* and the clematis 'Lasurstern' – an unforgettable combination this. Spectacular shrubs on both the walls and in the borders makes this an area of colour and interest the whole season. *Piptanthus laburnifolius,* with yellow pea-flowers and bright, shiny, evergreen trifoliate leaves, is one such plant, *Magnolia grandiflora* is another. *Ceanothus thyrsiflorus* gives a great splash of blue in early summer on one wall, near it is the excellent red of *Rosa moyesii* 'Geranium', another good association. The creamy, arched sprays of

Cytisus × *praecox* spread below the early roses *R. xanthina spontanea* 'Canary-Bird' and *R. hugonis* – an interesting mingling of yellows. A white-flowered hebe is planted near that invaluable summer shrub *Kolkwitzia amabilis.* And in a sheltered corner the 'Lobster Claw' *Clianthus puniceus* looks happy in the warmth of the wall and the shelter of the greenhouse.

The Shrub Garden is planted so that it is impossible to see across the comparatively small space it occupies, thus luring the visitor down the many curving paths and miniature beds, each with a theme of its own. For this is a garden of excitement, of bright and bold colours used skilfully and with good taste, of muted tones, soft colours and clever foliage contrast. And everywhere, the subtle treatment of the six dimensions in garden planning – colour, season, height, tone, texture and shape.

In one bed of the Shrub Garden is *Cotoneaster glaucophyllus,* a July flowerer and a late berrying plant. In another are some brooms: *Genista aetnensis,* the beautiful Etna Broom, a large and spreading shrub which can reach 6m. in height; the smaller, scented *G. cinerea,* and *G. virgata* from Madeira. On one corner is the viciously-thorned *Rosa sericea pteracantha,* unusual in having only four petals in its white flowers. *Pieris formosa forestii* grows well here, as does *Stephanadra tanakae,* a Japanese shrub with long arching deep-brown stems and greenish-white flowers, not unlike those of a spiraea, to which it is botanically allied: the leaves colour well in the autumn. A good association early in the year is *Rhododendron* 'Praecox' and *Primula amoena,* with bright violet-blue flowers.

In the Autumn Garden, one side is filled with a dahlia bed, that on the west-facing wall is largely devoted to heathers, while that on the near side contains larger shrubs. The arrangements here, and some of the plant associations, bear close inspection: *Buddleia davidii* 'White Cloud' as a backdrop to *Photinia villosa* – one of the best of autumn-colouring subjects, with bright-red fruits and vivid gold and scarlet leaves; *Pilostegia viburnoides,* a slow-growing evergreen clinging climber with narrow leathery leaves grows on the wall behind, with, next door to it, the Rose 'Allen Chandler', happily producing its lovely red flowers on this north-facing aspect: it has a double flowering period, early in the year and then again in September, with a bonus in the shape of magnificent orange-red hips in the autumn. A yucca adds contrast in texture and height. Euphorbias, the 1.2m. *E. wulfenii,* and the smaller vivid green-leaved *E.*

polychroma, add distinction, as this species always does. At the end is a sensational combination of the blue *Gentiana sino-ornata* against the red berries of *Cotoneaster* 'Hybridus Pendulus' (one of the best of the prostrate cotoneasters and a first-class groundcover), with *Erica vulgaris* 'C. W. Nix', which has deep-crimson flowers, and at the back a purple buddleia.

Doune: the Gardener's Cottage.

On leaving the Walled Garden by the south gate, ahead is the clear, rushing water of the burn, between close-cropped banks – a clever touch this, and quite right against the formality of the fine pinetum. On this south-facing outer wall of the garden grows *Hamamelis mollis*; *Jasminium nudiflorum*; *Viburnum farreri*, and a collection of *Chaenomeles* (*fragrans*) and other shrubs and roses.

Making one's way upstream, the scene widens to embrace a broad lawn running alongside the burn, reaching to the edge of the woods on the north side of the glen; here and there are island-beds planted with shrubs to create additional interest. A prominent feature is the Gardener's Cottage, a charming ornamental summer-house with a thatched roof. Looking back towards the west wall, two fine Tulip Trees, *Liriodendron tulipifera* catch the eye. These frame the west gate and in autumn the ground is yellow with their fallen leaves; against a backcloth of the bright red hips of *Rosa* 'Highdownensis' growing on the wall behind, they are a sensational sight, especially in combination with the brilliant blue of *Gentiana sino-ornata,* and *Calluna vulgaris* 'H. E. Beale' which are growing in a nearby bed.

The foundations of a collection of species rhododendrons also grow in this bed, along with a nurse crop of Scots Fir, to provide some protection for the young plants in this particularly exposed part of the Glen. Here too are a number of meconopsis, particularly the deepest of deep blue *M.* x *sheldonii,* which does well at Doune.

As indeed do the primulas. Sheets of these are planted beneath rhododendrons and other shrubs across the lawn. In a corner by the Gardener's Cottage is an effective association of a deep red rhododendron and the similar coloured *Primula pulverulenta.* Elsewhere are plantings of *PP. bulleyana, beesiana, helodoxa, nutans, capitata, vialii,* and the 'cowslip'-types *sikkimensis, florindae,* and *alpicola.*

The path now leads into the woodlands. Here are a number of fine trees, as well as some long-established rhododendrons, and some newer plantings of species and the better later-flowering hybrids. One unusual tree is *Crataegus lyalii,* an attractively shaped spreading specimen, but with flowers that smell like dead cats, which may account for its scarcity in cultivation! It is only the flowers, though, which smell so objectionable, the fruits are particularly fine, yellow and quite large. These banks and glades are a mass of bluebells in spring, but perhaps are at their most beautiful in the autumn with the colour of acers and sorbus – principally *S. hupehesis* and *S. sargentiana,* but there are also trees of the less usual *SS. ancuparia* 'Xanthocarpa', *decora* and *americana.* Magnolias, including *M. acuminata* and *M. obovata;* a Crested or Cock's Comb Beech, *Fagus sylvatica* 'Cristata'; a cut-leaf beech, *Fagus sylvatica heterophylla* – this one has a number of branches reverting to the common beech; walnuts; robinias, both *R.* x *hillieri* and *R. hispida,* the Rose Acacia from the South East United States; *Aesculus* x *carnea* 'Briotii' and many other interesting trees.

A particularly effective combination of plants may be seen by the bridge across the burn; here, against the ivy-covered stonework is the Skunk Lily, *Lysichitum (Lysichiton) americanum,* with a Stag's horn Sumach, *Rhus typhina* and a great grouping of the yellow *Primula florindae,* all beneath a fine, spreading, gnarled walnut tree. Much planting has gone on in the last few years in the Woodlands, of azaleas, primulas and other rhododendrons, a group of *Prunus maackii,* with shining gold-brown bark, and many other exciting plants.

The path leads back to the Pinetum and past many good rhododendrons. The early flowerers here are *R. oreodoxa,* more often than not nipped by the frost, but the later ones, among them *RR. fictolacteum, vernicosum, campanulatum* and the lilac-flowered *wallichii* all do well.

The Pinetum is particularly impressive, and pride of place must go to a magnificent Douglas Fir (*Pseudotsuga menziesii*) 45m. high at most recent reckoning. But there are others of equal distinction: nearby is a Nootka Cypress, *Chamaecyparis nootkatensis* of 30m. and a Lawson's Cypress, *Chamaecyparis lawsoniana* of 36m. In their shade is a delightful Japanese conifer, *Thujopsis dolabrata,* with somewhat flattened branches, and a Brewer's Weeping Spruce, *Picea brewerana.* A beautiful Incense cedar, *Calocedrus decurrens,* grows near the burn, and a good *Cryptomeria japonica* is planted near a majestic Wellingtonia, *Sequoiadendron giganteum,* this one a colossal 42m. tall. Quite close are two fine specimens of *Abies grandis,* the Great Fir, and *Abies procera,* the Noble Fir. At the back is a recent planting of rhododendrons designed to give extra colour before the roses in the Walled Garden reach their best. When they are established it will give even greater credence to Doune's fully-justified boast, that here is a garden for all seasons – and a most interesting one too.

How to get there

2 km west of DOUNE; 13 km north-west of STIRLING; 13 km east of CALLANDER

Off *A84 (DOUNE-CALLANDER Road)*.

TWELVE

Threave
(School of Practical Gardening)
Kirkcudbrightshire

THE INFLUENCE of Scottish gardeners on horticulture in this country has long been pronounced. Mention has already been made in this book to a number of Scots – authors, gardeners, and plant-hunters who in their way, did much to shape the gardening scene of their day. But there were many others, less well known except to specialist garden historians, who also made their mark.

Chief among these must rank James Loudon, the most distinguished and prolific, horticultural author of the first half of the nineteenth century and who, in 1826 founded the first gardening periodicial *The Gardener's Magazine and Register of Domestic Improvement* – one of a long line of books and magazines whose influence on horticulture in this country can hardly be exaggerated.

Before that, the 3rd Earl of Bute, a noted amateur botanist, and who had founded one of the earliest plant nurseries in Scotland, was largely instrumental in establishing Kew Gardens. Another Scot, was Philip Miller, who became Curator of the Physic Garden at Chelsea in 1722. He it was who set William Forsyth, a fellow-countryman (and after whom the genus *Forsythia* is named) on his gardening career; and it was on his advice that William Aiton, also a Scot, was appointed at Kew.

The great Scottish plant-collectors – Cunningham, Menzies, Douglas, Jeffrey and Forrest – have already been mentioned. But there were others of lesser importance, but who also found fame in their own small way. William Murray, who explored North West America after Menzies; Francis Masson, a widely travelled plant hunter who combed the Cape of Good Hope, the Canaries, Madeira, and the West Indies for plants before also turning his attention to

North America; William Kerr; and Robert Fortune, who scoured China in the latter half of the nineteenth century and brought back a number of excellent rhododendrons and other plants; to mention just a few.

These were great names in British horticulture, and all of Scottish origin, but it was the other Scottish gardeners, who made and have made the greatest and most lasting impact – those men who saw better chances of advancement across the Border, and who in a quiet, unheralded way, through their honesty, hard work and innate love of plants, became gardeners and head gardeners in many estates in England in the eighteenth and nineteenth centuries. So many, in fact, that Stephen Switzer, the landscape architect, in 1718 wrote: 'There are several Northern Lads, which whether they have serv'd time in their Art, or not, very few of us known anything of; yet by the help of a little Learning, and a great deal of Impudence they invade these Southern Provinces; and the natural benignity of this warmer climate has such wonderful influence on then, that one of them knows (or at least pretends to know) more in one twelve-month, than a laborious, honest *South* Country man does in seven years.'

This 'impudence' reached such an extreme when Scottish nurserymen began to make a success of their trade near London in the 1760s, that the resentment which had been bubbling for so long beneath the surface broke out. A long defunct corporate society was disinterred, and an embargo placed on the employment of Scottish lads – but the mood died and the influx of Scottish gardeners continued, to the ever-lasting benefit of gardening in this country, and by merit, they held their place.

And not only in England, for Thomas Blaikie, who was responsible for a large number of gardens in Switzerland and in France, was a chief exponent of the 'English Garden', then very popular on the Continent. A remarkable and vigorous man, he survived the last days of the *ancient régime* and the years of the French Revolution. In Russia, too a number of Scottish gardeners made their mark; their work and attitude widely respected.

When, in 1957, Major Allan Gordon left Threave, with a handsome legacy, to the National Trust for Scotland, it was with the express wish that the Trust should use his property for some worthwhile purpose. Originally it has been the intention of the Trust to

Threave: The Pinetum.

maintain Threave as a wildfowl reserve, and indeed the Threave Wildfowl Refuge where the many varieties of duck and sea-birds are frequent visitors is well-known on the British naturalist circuit. But in 1960 the Garden Committee of the National Trust for Scotland recommended that the estate be turned into a School for Practical Gardening. A decision which Major Gordon with his wide interests and concern for our heritage would have warmly welcomed. From that decisive moment the Threave Gardens under the capable and inspired direction of Bill Hean has gone from strength to strength. In the four years from 1971 attendance has nearly doubled, from a bare 20,000 or so to 37,000 in 1975. And rightly so, for Threave is fast becoming a national gardening 'must', a place of absorbing interest to any gardener.

The decline of the great estates in this country has meant that fewer and fewer boys have been able to gain that basic gardening training which is so essential to their craft – particularly in these days of highly commercial and scientific horticulture, not to say the extreme specialisation which is now accepted as a matter of course. Botanic Gardens, municipal parks, local authorities and the few private or company estates which exist, provide opportunity for the budding gardener, but economies both in style and manpower have lessened the breadth of horticultural experience which is available.

It is to help fill this need, to set on their professional road the successors of the great Scottish horticultural heritage, the heritage of Aiton, Miller, Forrest and Douglas, that the two-year course at the School of Practical Gardening at Threave is designed.

Every year seven students are enrolled, after thorough examination of both their physical and mental capability, to absorb to the full the benefits that Threave can offer them. Here, in conjunction with formal academic subjects, these gardeners of the future learn the rudiments of their trade. At the end of his two years' course the student takes a final examination and, hopefully, leaves Threave to find work in the expanding field of international horticulture.

When Threave came under the care of the National Trust for Scotland there was a walled-garden, a half hectare in extent, which contained a fine collection of the older type of apple trees, and a comprehensive collection of over 200 varieties of daffodils – but little else. The soil in this part of Kirkcudbrightshire is a heavy loam, inclined to water-log in winter and crack in drought – a rare enough event as the annual rainfall in this part of Scotland is 130cm. Here and there great outcrops of rock would break out and in many other places solid stone was not very far beneath the surface. Protected from the east and south-east by a great belt of trees, the garden gradually slopes to the west. Fine stands of timber, principally beech, but some oak, birch and conifers besides – break up the great swathes of grass to create glades and intriguing vistas. Here oceans of daffodils flowered in spring – still an unforgettable sight. Judicious clearing, shelter-belt planting and brilliant planning over an area which in all covers 28 hectares has created the opportunity for a garden designer's paradise. How cleverly this has been used the visitor must judge for himself.

The 500m. drive to the new Reception Centre at Threave is lined with a recent mixed planting of shrubs and trees – in their infancy now, but in four or five years they will create a most distinguished approach. On the ridge to the left a great belt of beech acts as windbreak from that quarter, and helps shelter the gardens from the cold winds off the Solway Firth.

It is beyond the Reception Centre that the *leitmotif* of Threave becomes apparent; the application of what was recently described as a combination of woodland garden, the garden glade and the island

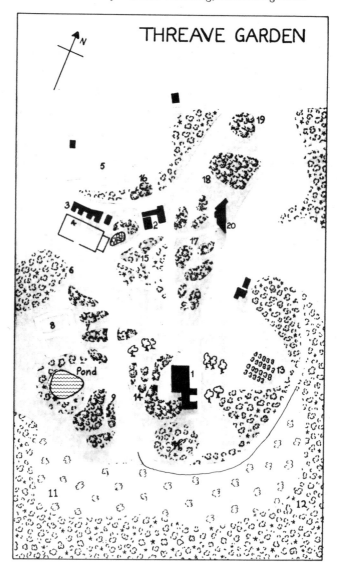

THREAVE GARDEN

Pond

1. Threave House
2. Stables
3. Greenhouses
4. Walled Garden
5. Nursery
6. Peat Garden
7. Rock Garden
8. Vegetable Garden
9. Heath Garden
10. Pinetum
11. Arboretum
12. Wood
13. Orchard
14. Herbaceous Beds
15. Woodland Garden
16. Winter Border
17. Rose Garden
18. Crab and Cherry Collection
19. Bog Garden
20. Reception

21 Threave in Spring

22 *top* Threave. The Pinetum. Beneath the gravel lies thick black polythene

23 *above* Threave. A corner of the patio, with Celmisia and *Clematis chrysocoma sericea* much like *C. montana* but with larger white flower

bed. And it is intensely interesting to see these styles – some of the contemporary adaptations of the Robinson, the Jekyll, the Crathes schools. Some, to me, are a success – on the whole the grander ones with perhaps an edge conforming with an existing feature; others look bitty, unworthy and out of place, dwarfed by their surroundings. But that is the intention behind Threave: the many styles on display are intended to cover a spectrum of designs and ideas, some will be controversial, few will suit all tastes or all situations, but everywhere at Threave is a feast for thought.

One series of beds which are a great success are the shrub and species rose borders beyond the Reception Centre. On a heavily-contoured area sloping to the west down to the Woodland Garden and the Walled Garden beyond irregular beds of varying sizes and varying shapes have been cut. Well represented in these are the Scotch or Burnet roses, *Rosa spinosissima* (*pimpinellifolia*), which will grow in the poorest soil but have a distressingly short flowering season; although they make up for this to some extent by an attractive, tight-knit foliage and decorative hips. Hybrid Tea and Floribunda and other shrub roses have been added to create interest and extend the flowering period of these beds. It is worth noting how well the sparse texture of leaf of the yellow rambler 'Goldfinch' shows up against the heavier leafing of the spinosissima and shrub roses. The hardy stand-bys of Rose 'Fruhlingsgold', 'Nevada', the rugosa 'Blanc Double de Coubert' are interspersed with an excellent range of old and modern shrub roses including the very beautiful 'Koenigin von Danemarck' (Queen of Denmark) of the richest pink and the dark purple moss rose 'Captain J. Ingram', and a variety of underplantings, many with grey leaves have been tried.

The Woodland Garden is full of fine shrubs beneath a canopy of larch, beech, Douglas (*Pseudotsuga menziesii*) and Silver Firs (*Abies alba*) – it is worth noticing the paths which are composed of sawdust over clinker, remain virtually weed-free and only require annually a topping up of sawdust by way of maintenance. Here are a number of trees of *Magnolia wilsonii* with pendulous saucer-shaped white flowers and a central mass of red stamens – but one needs to be a contortionist to appreciate their beauty to the full in a young plant. A number of rhododendrons grow here including *R. souliei*, *R. oreotrephes* of the triflorum series, a Forrest introduction, *R. bureavii* with dark glossy green leaves and a rich red indumentum beneath, the young shoots which are an eye-catching grey (this species has a tight truss of rose-coloured flowers with darker markings), and a number of hybrids including the dark red 'Spitfire' and perhaps the most widely known and planted 'Pink Pearl' which received an Award of Merit as long ago as 1897.

Choisya ternata, the aromatic-leaved Mexican Orange, is here growing happily in half shade, with hydrangeas, viburnums and many other shrubs and desirable trees. The ground-cover plants are of particular merit and worthy of a lot of study. Conspicuous is a bright-green rubus with long trailing red-bristly stems, *R. tricolor.* The herbaceous *Clematis recta* with fresh grey-green leaves spreads unstaked along one path. *Mitella caulescens* a member of the saxifrage family is another useful but little used subject for this purpose. To add colour and interest, great sheets of candelabra primulas, foxgloves (the Excelsior strain), hostas and veratrum vie with tree peonies and lilies, *L. martagon* and *L.* x *hollandicum* (*L. umbellatum*) in particular. A simple but effective combination is the green *Euphorbia wulfenii* growing through the common periwinkle *Vinca minor.*

On the slope behind the crow-stepped, castellated pile of Threave House are some new plantings in island beds of rhododendrons, azaleas and *Kalmia angustifolia,* with specimen trees in each – sorbus principally including *S. vilmorinii* and the lesser-known *S. pluripinnata,* but there are also specimens of *Stranvaesia davidiana* and a cultivar of our native Bird Cherry, *Prunus padus* 'Purple Queen'.

The rhododendrons include 'Blue Tit' perhaps the best of the early blues, 'Elizabeth' the griersonianum hybrid of a strong dark red, 'Scarlet O'Hara' another deep red (here set among a pink azalea), and the pure white *R.* 'White Lady'. Above is the Orchard and the continuation of the great beech belt on the ridge above the garden, the perfect background to what promises to be a most effective planting.

Continuing on one's way above Threave House, in the great glen are some small beds, incongruous though they might appear in the great green expanse, the plant associations here are of particular note. Hollies are the prevailing feature – the striking *Ilex aquifolium* 'Golden Queen', *I.a.* 'Argenteomarginata' with white-margined leaves and *I.* x *altaclarensis* 'Hodginsii' with purple stems among others. The experimental underplantings include *Cotoneaster horizontalis* and other prostrate cotoneasters, the variegated periwinkle *Vinca major* 'Variegata' ('Elegantissima') and most effective of all, the small white-flowered, glaucous-leaved *Hebe pinguifolia* 'Pagei' which used to be known as *Hebe pageana*.

At the furthest, the southern end of the garden, lies the Arboretum containing a wealth of young and interesting trees. The purple-leaved *Acer platanoides* 'Crimson King' always causes comment, but equally dominant in their season are some of the excellent collection of sorbus which is something of à speciality at Threave. The more common are well represented but some others are noteworthy and unusual, including *S. pseudoferica*; the Pyrennean *S. mougeotii* with whitish-grey undersides to the leaf and quite long red fruits in the autumn; the British native *S. bristoliensis* which hails from the Avon Gorge near Bristol and has orange fruits; and *S. hedlundii* from Sikkim, a sparkling white when the wind ruffles its great elliptical leaves sometimes 30 cm. or more long.

Below the Arboretum stands the Pinetum of dwarf conifers, stark against their beds of light-grey gravel. This is laid on a covering of thick black polythene and the trees then planted through it. Testing labour-saving ideas is very much the intention at Threave and this has certainly proved its worth for only wind-borne seeds will grow in the gravel, and they can be rapidly, surely and painlessly removed.

Now turning for home, we pass the Heather Garden. Planted in 1965, over the succeeding years a very comprehensive collection of heathers has now been established. To break the monotony of their contour a number of larger trees and shrubs are growing in the beds, birches, a rowan – the 'Enchanted Tree' of the Gaelic – acers and others. Great use is made of the low, spreading silver-grey 'Woolly Willow' *Salix lanata*.

To the right of the main path can now be seen the Herbaceous Beds below the house. The planting schemes, and particularly the treatment of heights is deserving of especial examination. From ground level the effect is of cleverly executed sweeps of colour almost filling an area that cries to be filled. But from above, the whole is seen to be fixed within the context of the glades and surrounding trees, and it can be discerned that the beds themselves are in fact comparatively small.

A great many herbaceous plants are used; aquilegias, astilbes, the pea-flowered *Galega officinalis,* the great grey hairy leaves of *Salvia turkestanica*. Irises and hemerocallis provide a differing tone and texture, and one whole bed is devoted to seedling kniphofias. Particularly effective is a combination of purple sage *Salvia officinalis*

'Purpurascens', a deep purple member of the thistle family *Circium rivulare* 'Atropurpureum', *Atriplex hortensis* 'Atrosanguinea' the purple orache, and *Stachys macrantha* 'Rosea'.

At the back of the borders against a wall of the terrace are some good shrubs: *Kolkwitzia amabilis,* the well-named *Olearia stellulata* 'Splendens', *Viburnum x burkwoodii* and another viburnum, a variant of our common Guelder Rose, *V. opulus* 'Compactum', and one of the best of all variegated shrubs *Weigela florida* 'Variegata'. But, originally, the shrubs are not permitted to overlap to the lawn edge, instead bays are created for bearded iris cultivars. The contrast in tone with their immediate background is peculiarly effective. And, to continue the surprises which Threave has to offer, two pendulous willow-leaved pears, *Pyrus salicifolia* 'Pendula'; but, instead of being treated in a conventional manner and allowed to droop unhindered, here a leader is tortured upright and the tree allowed to grown in tiers to create a narrow cascade of silver-grey.

A mixed shrub planting leads towards the Pond. Formerly a boggy hollow it was excavated and lined with eight inches of wet clay; the result is an impervious lining. In this area can be found the Siberian *Caragana arborescens,* with yellow pea-like flowers, a tough and obliging plant, *Stranvaesia davidiana undulata* a low-growing shrub with crimson berries in season and several *Viburnum plicatum* 'Mariesii' with horizontal branches. A number of specimen trees have been planted including the White Poplar, *Populus alba.* This is a peaceful, secluded spot, sheltered by a good stand of beech on the higher ground behind; to the west there is a fine view across Galloway. The pond surrounds are planted with iris, *Caltha palustris, Primula denticulata,* with one or two particularly fine forms, and, foxgloves. A useful, quick-growing, though otherwise singularly characterless shrub, well-named the Groundsel Tree, is *Baccharis patagonica* from the Magellan Straits and accordingly wholly hardy. It can grow up to 3m. and is a useful windbreak. Its greatest attraction is its name which is derived from Bacchus, the God of Wine, because of a supposed winey smell of its roots.

The Rock Garden was almost the first area to be developed when the estate was taken over by the National Trust for Scotland. Use was made of a great, natural outcrop of rock, supplemented by other boulders where needed. To counteract the heavy nature of the indigenous soil, screes and pockets of lighter soil have been added and many fine alpines now flourish here. Imaginative use has been made of contour-creating conifers and a number of low-growing shrubs incorporated into the planting scheme to provide additional character.

On the way to the Peat Garden one passes *Fabiana imbricata* 'Prostrata' a rather heath-like shrub forming a dense mound of branches covered in pale mauve flowers in May and June. This form is said to be somewhat hardier than the type.

The Peat Garden is full of delightful plants in an area where extensive use has been made of peat walls, from local peat, an idea which originated at Logan Gardens near Stranraer and was further developed at the Royal Botanic Garden, Edinburgh. It is now an extremely popular and practical way of constructing peat beds. In the Peat Garden is a particularly fine collection of primulas, not least *P. vialii,* a notoriously choosy doer. Many of the dwarf rhododendrons originated from Gigha, where it has been the policy of the National Trust for Scotland to send the larger species and hybrids to Brodick Castle Gardens while the smaller varieties will be grown here. Among the rhododendrons can be seen a number of other shrubs and plants of interest; the evergreen *Gaultheria antipoda* from New Zealand flourishes in the moist peaty soil: it has attractive lily-of-the valley-like white flowers in June and July– the cruciform herbaceous *Dentaria digitata* with rich purple flowers; the orchid-like roscoeas are represented by the yellow *R. cautleoides* and the violet-purple *R. humeana.* Another eye-catching plant is the tiny-leaved, slow-growing holly, *Ilex crenata* 'Convexa' with glossy convex leaves. There are also many ericaceous plants, cassiopes, vacciniums and the charming dwarf shrub *Rhodothamus chamaecistus* which rarely grows higher than 25cm and has pale rose, very flat slightly rhododendron-like flowers. Pride of place must, however, go to the expanding collection of nomocharis with their flat lily-like flowers, the envy of most gardens in the south. Striking are the yellow *N. oxypetala* and the beautiful, clear pink, crimson-spotted *N. pardanthina.* In complete contrast is a cross-section of ferns growing in small beds made of oak logs.

The borders below the high south wall of the Walled Garden are home to a mixed representative planting of every type of plant, from bulb to shrub to climber. Round the corner is one of the most recent developments at Threave, the Patio, which was constructed in 1972. This is a place of great charm and clever design: the use of paving, great and small, deserves especial study. Pride of place here is given to a small wispy tree of the Weeping Aspen, *Populus tremula* 'Pendula' a constantly shimmering plant which gives a curiously restful perpetual motion. The planting also deserves close inspection, particularly the wall planting where some clever plant associations have been incorporated: a berberis with the orange-flowered *Eccremocarpus scaber* growing through it; *Pyracantha rogersiana* 'Flava' with a front planting of *Hebe macrantha* with its leathery, toothed leaves and disproportionately large but lovely white flowers. The architectural scope of the lanceolate grey-silver leaves of *Celmisia coriacea* is clearly brought home. In a corner against the paving it is an immediate eye-stopper. *Clematis chrysocoma sericea* (*C. spooneri*) somewhat like the better-known *C. montana* but with larger white flowers, grows against the wall with some plants of Inverewe's Madeiran geranium *G. anemonifolium* at its foot.

Within the Walled Garden are, as might be expected, superbly-grown beds of fruit, vegetables and herbs. The greenhouses and propagating frames are well worth a visit – especially the odd corners which house a number of unusual and exciting plants. Behind and beyond the Winter Border, which is devoted to plants which give value in winter either through leaf, flower or coloured stem, is the Nursery. This is always a source of attraction and there is a continuing demonstration of hedging plants.

And so back to the Reception Centre, but in passing the Stable Block, a deep pink climbing rose should be noted. This is the Bourbon 'Madame Isaac Pereire', an incomparable rose with huge blooms of an almost overwhelming and delightful fragrance. More usually grown as a shrub rose where it can reach 2 metres, possibly as a climber, the heavy flowers are to be seen at their best.

Beyond the Reception Centre, is a planting of ornamental cherries and malus, with an underplanting of daffodils to give yet another spring attraction. Beyond that again is a newly created bog garden, and, by the time this book is produced, yet more innovations and developments will doubtless be added to the many fascinations of this remarkable garden.

For although Threave is primarily intended as a School of gardening (where day classes are also held for amateurs) the achievement is far more than that. Already in terms of visitors the estate has proved one of the most popular gardens owned by the National Trust for Scotland. It is totally different in concept to any other, and inside what was virtually only a landscaped shell it has been possible both to construct a garden and to experiment in garden design and plant association. The result is that Threave is a treasure-house of thought-provoking ideas, particularly for the owner of the smaller garden. This is a function sometimes overlooked when one sees, admires and enjoys some of the very beautiful and older-established gardens described in the pages of this book.

How to get there

3 km west of CASTLE DOUGLAS; 30 km south-west of DUMFRIES. Off   *A75*   (CASTLE-DOUGLAS–GATEHOUSE   OF   FLEET   Road)

Some Other Scottish Gardens

NOTE The gardens listed below are open for extended, but various periods. To avoid disappointment, intended visitors are advised to consult the Scottish Tourist Board or the publication mentioned in the Introduction which is produced by Scotland's Garden Scheme, 26 Castle Terrace, Edinburgh, and is obtainable at most newsagents. The numbers correspond with those on the 'Garden Map of Scotland' on page 9.

1. **Abercairny** (W. S. H. Drummond Moray Esq) Crieff, Perthshire (Tayside).
   A very extensive garden with many fine old trees. Vast herbaceous borders and woodland garden. Lilacs, daffodils, rhododendrons, azaleas, primulas, meconopsis.
2. **Achamore House** (D. W. N. Landale Esq) Isle of Gigha, Argyll (Strathclyde).
   World famous garden, home of many semi-tropical plants. Renowned for rhododendrons, camellias, primulas and many other subjects.
3. **An Cala** (Mrs Blakeney) Easdale, Argyll (Strathclyde).
   A beautifully planned and planted garden. Roses, azaleas, and other excellent and interesting plants.
4. **Ardanaiseig** (Mr & Mrs J. M. Brown) Kilchrenan, Argyll (Strathclyde).
   Fine views and autumn colour. Rhododendrons and many unusual trees, shrubs and other plants.
5. **Ardwell House** (Mr & Mrs J. Brewis) Ardwell, Stranraer, Wigtownshire (Dumfries & Galloway).
   Within a few kilometres of the Logan Botanic Gardens. Excellent rhododendrons and azaleas, spring bulbs and autumn colouring.
6. **Calgary House** (Mrs Eric Mackenzie) Isle of Mull, Argyll (Island of Mull).
   Home of many exotic shrubs and trees.
7. **Craignish Castle** (Mrs Platts Mills) Ardfern, Argyll (Strathclyde). Well known for its very fine rhododendrons.
8. **Crarae Lodge** (Sir Ilay Campbell of Succoth, Bt.) by Inveraray, Argyll (Strathclyde).
   Famous rhododendron, tree and shrub garden. Brilliant autumn colours. A garden for all seasons, and a very notable one.
9. **Drummond Castle** (the Earl of Ancaster) Crieff, Perthshire (Tayside).
   Famous formal Italian garden with magnificent parterres, a staggering sight at any season of the year. Superb trees, rose garden, banks of azaleas and shrubs – all on a colossal scale.

10. **Edinburgh: The Royal Botanic Gardens**
World famous Botanic Gardens, renowned for its superb rock garden, outstanding rhododendron collection and many other features including a new plant house and heather garden.

11. **Glenarn** (Mr & Mrs A. C. Gibson) Rhu, Dunbartonshire (Strathclyde).
One of the outstanding gardens in Scotland, noted for its rhododendrons, magnolias, and other shrubs. Lilies and nomocharis particularly fine.

12. **Hopetoun House** (The Trustees for Hopetoun House) South Queensferry, West Lothian (Lothian).
Magnificent grounds and deer park a fine background for one of Scotland's noblest houses. Formal rose garden, and some splendid trees.

13. **Keir** (Lt-Col William Stirling of Keir) Dunblane, Perthshire (Central).
Huge and extremely fine garden. Shrubs and herbaceous borders, rhododendrons and daffodils, glades of azaleas and many other features.

14. **Kildrummy Castle** (Kildrummy Castle Garden Trustees) Alford, Strathlon, Aberdeenshire (Grampian).
Famous Japanese water garden. Excellent shrubs and trees.

15. **Kinmount** (Hoddom & Kinmount Estates) Annan, Dumfriesshire (Dumfries & Galloway).
A fine woodland garden.

16. **Leith Hall** (National Trust for Scotland) Kennethmont, Aberdeenshire (Grampian).
Excellent herbaceous borders, the catmint sweep a memorable sight. Rock garden. Unusual Pictish stones.

17. **Lochinch & Castle Kennedy Gardens** (the Earl of Stair) Stranraer, Wigtownshire (Dumfries & Galloway).
Landscaping on the grand scale. Avenues of enormous monkey-puzzles and other trees. Massed rhododendrons and azaleas. A botanical and general gardening paradise.

18. **Logan Botanic Gardens** Stranraer, Wigtownshire (Dumfries & Galloway).
Famous Botanic Garden, noted for its many rare trees and shrubs in an almost semi-tropical setting. Eleven separate gardens, each a delight in itself. Magnificent drifts of meconopsis.

19. **Malleny** (National Trust for Scotland) Balerno, Nr Edinburgh (Lothian).
A garden of great charm. Shrub roses a speciality.

20. **Pollok Park, Glasgow**
Full of valuable trees and shrubs. Unique collection of rhododendrons. Terrace and alpine gardens. Natural woodlands.

21. **Scone Palace** (the Earl of Mansfield) Perth (Tayside).
One of the oldest and probably the most famous Pinetum in Scotland dating from 1848. Woodland gardens and attractive walks. Remains of the old Abbey of Scone.

22. **Strone** (Lord & Lady Glenkinglas) Cairndow, Argyll (Strathclyde).
Fine Pinetum, and other trees and shrubs. Woodland garden, flowering cherries, rhododendron and a colossal *Abies alba*.

23. **The House on the Shore** (Capt. J. B. Blackett) Arbigland, Kirkbean, Dumfries Kirkudbrightshire (Dumfries & Galloway).
Fine woodlands and formal garden in a delightful setting.

24. **Williamston** (W. T. H. Haughton Esq) Insch, Aberdeenshire (Grampian).
A garden of great charm and many features. Red-foliage plants a speciality.

25. **Younger Botanic Gardens, Benmore** (Strathclyde).
Exceptionally fine woodlands and rhododendrons. A haven of rare and tender trees; excellent conifers and a memorable avenue of sequoias. Many other features.

General Index

Index of Plants